Millionairess

Millionairess

Self-Made Women of America

Lois Rich-McCoy

HARPER & ROW, PUBLISHERS

NEW YORK, HAGERSTOWN, SAN FRANCISCO, LONDON

FIRST EDITION

Designed by Lydia Link

Library of Congress Cataloging in Publication Data

Rich-McCoy, Lois.
  Millionairess.
  1. Millionairesses—United States—Biography.
I. Title.
HF5386.R49 1978   338'.092'2 [B]   78-2142
ISBN 0-06-012852-6

78 79 80 81 82 10 9 8 7 6 5 4 3 2 1

Millionairess is the result of the love, cooperation, and respect my husband and I share. I believe the time-honored thought "Behind every successful individual is another" has validity; no one—male or female—can succeed without support and appreciation. I therefore dedicate this book to my greatest critic and staunchest admirer, my ablest consultant, my partner in life—

to FLOYD W. McCOY, JR.

Si qua voles apte nubere nube pari.
—OVID

Contents

Acknowledgments

I WISH TO EXPRESS MY GRATITUDE TO: Rusty Lotti; Michael Miles; Paul LoGerfo; Zimmy; Anne Erickson; Beatrice Agnew, of the Palisades Free Library; the Trembleys; Paul Gilbert; my parents, Ruth and Harry Rich; friends who cared for Brent and Elana during my travels; R. Andrew Boose; the Woods Hole Library staff; the Finklestein Library research staff; Mark Morris; fellow airline passengers on dozens of planes offering companionship, conversation, and comments; and Albert Sturdivant, who without knowing my name loaned me a credit card to ease a 2–4 A.M. flight layover. (And my apologies for losing his address and never returning it.)

I am particularly in debt to each of the outstanding women in this volume who offered hospitality and shared their life stories, personal thoughts, disappointments, and dreams. This giving of themselves was complemented by interviews with the individuals surrounding them: spouses and friends, parents and children, professional associates, competitors, and employees—all vital to the writing of *Millionairess*.

"Whatever women do they must do twice as well as men to be thought half as good. Luckily, this is not difficult."

—Charlotte Whitton

Preface

On the Creation of Millionairess

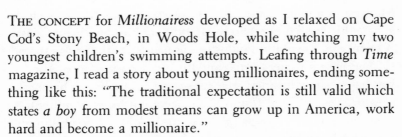

THE CONCEPT for *Millionairess* developed as I relaxed on Cape Cod's Stony Beach, in Woods Hole, while watching my two youngest children's swimming attempts. Leafing through *Time* magazine, I read a story about young millionaires, ending something like this: "The traditional expectation is still valid which states *a boy* from modest means can grow up in America, work hard and become a millionaire."

I thought, What about a *girl?* Toying with the concept of Horatio Alger heroines, I mentioned the thesis of the book to acquaintances. A common comment was "You'll never find twelve women who rose to the top, who neither inherited nor married wealth, but were financially and professionally successful in their own right." My friends were wrong. I found thirty; I could have found a hundred and thirty.

Dreamers, mystics, philosophers, poets, relax. Although the twelve females are indeed wealthy, they are also self-satisifed human beings. I was surprised to find I liked each of these personable millionaires, who are straight-speaking and logical with a touch of unexpected dreaminess, and loaded with specialized and generalized information. Although some are not attractive in the traditional sense, I found them to be fine-looking people, with pleased expressions, rather Cheshire-catlike.

Interviewing the ladies (none of whom, to my knowledge, minds being called a lady) was a pleasure. They had so much to say that in most cases my prepared questions and subject-matter discussion plans never had to be referred to. Usually after hours of conversation, I would pull out my notebook to see if there was anything else I'd like to know, and find that all my queries had been taken care of without my having to make them.

When these women were initially reached about arrangements for interviews, they praised the book's concept. One, from the Midwest, thought it fine that I was searching for subjects in geographic areas other than the traditional East and West Coasts. A woman in the fashion industry was pleased with the age spread; the youngest is in her thirties and the oldest past seventy. Another was happy show-business successes were not included; having no theatrical talent, she found their accomplishments difficult to relate to. A fourth was glad the volume would not be philosophical; she felt readers were past that plateau. The time was right for models, not rhetoric.

The women featured in this volume exemplify the feats unshackled women can accomplish. But remember that this group made their own freedom and individually had the drive and guts to get what they personally wanted out of life. They are inspirational to women floundering in a world which now allows them to achieve yet offers few tangible methodical clues.

An author's opinions cannot be separated from her writing. I did, however, try neither to judge nor analyze these women, their lives and their principles, nor reach conclusions. As my editor, Hugh Van Dusen, aptly put it, "Good stories well told will have plenty of message on their own. . . . The lessons will be evident to the reader."

So be it.

Lois Rich-McCoy

Palisades, New York

Millionairess

1

EARTH MOTHER
Vera Neumann

————•••⟨∞⟩•••————

THE TINY sixty-nine-year-old woman kindles nostalgic remembrances of a favorite aunt: comfortable pantsuit, smile-creased face, perfect blond salon coif, a trifle tongue-tied . . . one sees a sensible-looking lady with the delicacy of her youth still evident. But this particular five-foot female contains a surprise. The abstract-design ornament pinned to her blouse is a tipoff; pleasant aging matrons do not wear the brass jewelry of Alexander Calder.

World-known simply as "Vera," this co-chairman of the board of the Vera Industries—retail sales over a hundred million dollars—and a director of parent corporation Manhattan Industries (the Manhattan Shirt people purchased Vera, Inc., for more than five million dollars over a decade ago) is a bewildering combination of textile artist, manufacturer, corporate officer, and Jewish-grandma type.

The many facets of Vera Neumann were evident about six years ago when a bedsheet manufacturer decided to utilize Vera designs. A meeting was held to discuss patterns. Thomas Costello, president of the Vera companies, describes Neumann's encounter with the corporate heads of Burlington Industries after being flown South in the bedding corporation's jet. (Remember this is a woman, born in 1909, barely sixty inches tall, with a hesitant manner of speech, who looks like everyone's conception of a modern grandma.) "Here we are in this room with about ninety-five guys who probably look just like me only maybe a little bit older, and they all are geniuses from the factory. . . . They are telling why everything couldn't be done. . . ." Complex problems arose—size, color, pattern repeats, positioning—in converting a painting on paper to a design printed by a rotary yard-goods machine that would ultimately produce decorated flat sheets, coordinated pillowcases, as well as bottom-fitted sheets, in four sizes, plus bath towels, hand towels, and washcloths. The Burlington group saw only impossible problems as they considered Neumann's artistic offerings. Costello relates: "So Vera sat there very calmly. . . . She redid all the things, and readapted some of them . . . so it could work on the equipment." The marriage of Burlington bedding with Vera prints was successful. Today, Burlington's Vera patterns are the top-selling designer sheets.

Thomas Costello, Holy Cross graduate who says he didn't have the fare to go to Harvard, is a distinguished-looking, immaculately dressed New York City corporate executive with movie-star gray hair, gray vested suit, and diagonally striped tie. The visual and personality combination of Costello and Neumann as a working team stretches the imagination. Equally hard to envision is Vera teamed with Perry Ellis, the young understated beautiful male who creates clothing under the Vera trademarks "Portfolio" and "Very Vera." Sophisticated, and subtle, Ellis states that, as "one artistic person working with another," designing with Vera is ". . . a pleasure; Vera understands the aesthetics of life. . . . She has an earth quality, a motherliness . . . that's the overriding thing with her. . . . If she likes you, she envelops you, in a sense of family . . . like your Aunt Rose, like a member of her family. You begin to feel like a close relative, particularly if you work with her on a day-to-day basis." Ellis respects the artist in Neumann as he feels warmth for the woman who makes him want to laugh— "You don't want to be philosophical with a dear aunt"—and points out that, at the same time, she has a very strong ego about her work which he considers to be valid.

Vera Neumann feels differently; she says she has an inferiority complex. Yet her childhood was filled with security, acceptance, and encouragement.

The product of a stable, laughter-filled family life, Vera Salaff was born in Stamford, Connecticut, the third child of four. Ignoring the Jewish tradition of naming children after dead relatives, Vera's mother, who loved to read, chose to name each of her four children after a literary character. The oldest daughter, Alice, was named for Alice in Wonderland; the namesake of the second sister, Grace Aguilar Salaff, was an English writer born of Spanish parents; Philip Marston Salaff, the youngest child, says he was named for an obscure English poet. Neumann finds it ironic that her mother named her for a historic "women's libber" and, Vera's brother says, Russian feminist Vera Bashkirtseff, who also was known by only one name: Vera.

Vera Salaff's mother, Fanny, was an intellectual. Prior to the birth of her first child, Mrs. Salaff purchased a piano and learned to play so the infant Alice might appreciate fine music from birth. Fanny—with her husband—instilled a high degree of self-confidence in all their four children. Although singing on stage was not a profession for a young lady in the 1930s, it was Alice's choice, and her parents encouraged her. Meyer Salaff did draw the line, however, when his daughter was invited to sing for the

Shubert Brothers in New York City; well-brought-up young ladies simply did not perform in that town. Grace, the next child, was a pianist; Philip studied to be an engineer, at that time a difficult profession for a Jewish boy to enter.

Stamford, Connecticut, was in many ways an odd place for the family to reside. As one of only a handful of Jewish families in the Yankee town at a time when people openly and blatantly remarked on immigrant-sounding names, Vera's father hung a large "Salaff" sign over his coffee- and tea-importing business. He and his wife were from Russia. While the mother was serious, yet loving and openly affectionate, Vera's father—who set aside a room filled with books which the delighted children entered on Sundays when he escorted them in—was intelligent, if not as intellectual as his wife. Vera says he was a playful, cheerful, laughing person. Her eyes light up as she remembers: "He would play with a group of kids in the neighborhood, play a game with them . . . he would tie a sandbag at the end of a rope and swing it around and we were all supposed to jump over it. He played with everyone on the block."

A follower of Socialist Eugene Debs, Salaff ran unsuccessfully for a town office. Yet Vera remembers that he never seemed serious and she blames that trait, along with his cheerful spirit, for his business failures. Though he was not a success financially his household provided a nourishing environment for the children and encouraged them to utilize their various talents.

Alice remembers her younger sister's dabbling in the arts at a very young age, lying on a rug with a paintbrush and crayon. "Each day she drew from memory whatever impressed her . . . from the smallest fiddlehead fern to a giant sunflower," and the teachers directed her from one classroom to the next, from kindergarten to eighth grade, chalking the "flower of the month" on each blackboard.

The family lived in Connecticut until the stock-market crash, when Salaff lost his business, then moved to New York City where Vera attended Cooper Union Art School at night. She continued for the next nine years.

While working for a Seventh Avenue fashion house, she met a man—a decorator—and they became engaged. He introduced her to the home-furnishings field and she started to design furniture and accessory motifs. At some point she realized the relationship was not a healthy one. Vera today seems slightly uncomfortable trying to describe the problem: "It turned out to be sort of a mixture of one way or the other . . . which at that point I was so naïve I didn't understand." Neumann is trying to say he was bisexual. "I decided in time . . . I never *could* understand why he was entertaining me and his male friends at the same time." She laughs. "He was a decorator, very sensitive, artistic." Vera is not critical: "After all, what makes us right and makes their behavior wrong?"

Continuing to work in home-furnishings design, she began dating a rather idealistic man and they became close. He died fighting in the Spanish Civil War. While Vera has difficulty remembering names, and has been known to forget the name of a person with whom she has been associated for decades, she does remember his. Years later she named her son after him.

She met her husband-to-be, George Neumann, at "just a very ordinary party." An immigrant from Vienna, George Neumann, loaded with self-esteem, was suited to Vera emotionally, intellectually, and artistically. When he was a young boy, the Nazis had entered his family's apartment. George announced they could not take his mother and father, who were old and sick, and pointed out that he was too young to be of any use to them. As he grew older, he never could understand why they listened to him. A friend in the United States managed to make arrangements so the child and his parents could enter this country before the war.

When George met Vera, he was working for a Long Island aviation plant, with a deferred war status. "We lived together for a long time," confides Vera. He moved into her studio and they spent many hours discussing art, architecture, and graphic theory. Vera's freethinking suffragette mother thought it wonderful that the two young people were sharing an apartment; she considered it a sensible arrangement, according to Vera. (Keep in mind we are discussing the 1940s.) Her father agreed with Fanny Salaff's view, because, says Vera, "he liked George." Vera Neumann, whose voice is reminiscent of Edith Bunker's, tends to garble her thoughts in speech. Of this arrangement, she said, "Yes, it was very unusual at that time. But at that time everyone was living together."

This arrangement lasted five years, while Vera worked as a free-lance artist. At about the time World War II ended, they decided to begin their own business. Vera Saloff, who spelled the name differently from her parents, and George Neumann searched for an inexpensive work space. As they were shown an area in an old building in Manhattan, the landlord told them that Henry Luce had used that space to begin *Life* magazine. A believer in omens, Vera decided to rent it, and to marry. Vera says the wedding took place because the newly formed business necessitated travel which was awkward for an unwed couple. Vera Saloff Neumann was thirty-four.

The thought was to begin a textile-printing concern—it was George's family's business in Europe—and their first design was to be a painting of Vera's. She brushed directly on a silk screen and, as she always did with her artwork, signed her name in the bottom corner. After a moment's thought, she decided to add a little something else near her signature. She painted a small ladybug. Today that insect is the Vera logo.

They placed a kitchen table in their "factory," and together Vera and George screened, spreading ink onto the middle of the silk and, with a squeegee, distributing the paint, using even pressure across the silk-screened pattern. As the paint oozed through to make Vera's pattern appear on a place mat, the signature she had placed in the bottom left-hand corner was also transferred. This, according to Vera, was the first instance of a designer-signed article.

While Vera touts herself as first, she does not believe that her signature or other designers' names help the product to sell except to a small segment of the population. "Now of course there are some people . . . who look at the names first. Like those people who carry Gucci bags. It's a status kind of thing, and if you can say that you have a this or a that in your home . . . well!" If asked why she continues to place a signature on her products, she sidesteps, and again relates how her first attempts ended with "Vera" emblazoned on them. Department-store personnel do not agree with Vera's analysis. A buyer with the Florida-based Burdine's states, "Vera scarves are often requested at Christmas. . . ." A department manager at New Jersey's Bamberger's commented: "Scarves by Vera are very popular; many customers ask for them by name."

Vera Neumann did not initially produce scarves.

The first articles sold were place mats. She designed and, with George, carried out the printing process. They named their business Printex and, because they were floundering financially, teamed up with F. Werner Hamm, who invested in the small company and acted as salesman. Still associated with Vera Industries, Mr. Hamm is co-chairman of the board with Vera.

The place mats were selling but it was difficult to obtain linen fabric when, unexpectedly, in this postwar period, a surplus of silk developed from parachute production. The only silk scarves available in the United States were imported from Europe and were expensive; Vera Neumann thought it made sense to produce scarves here. They began manufacturing low-cost scarves—under five dollars—printing in single colors using two hues, the simplest silk-screening operation. By superimposing two shades, a third was created. A trio of colors thereby resulted from two screenings.

The selling of under-five-dollar scarves did not activate enough sales for the company to continue to grow; in addition, surplus parachute-silk supplies were diminishing. Vera's company decided to approach prestigious F. Schumacher & Co., renowned for their exclusive wallpaper and fabric patterns. The firm agreed to buy as much of the Vera-design fabric as was available as long as Vera Neumann adapted the pattern shown to Schumacher as a repetitive design. The resultant volume of business necessitated a switch to automatic silk-screening machines.

As Vera continued to design, her name became recognizable to women throughout the United States. The Vera signature became familiar enough to appear in a 1966 *Herald Tribune* crossword puzzle; five across requested a four-letter word for "Designer of scarves and table linens."

Her designs had and have a simple, fresh, clean quality, bright with bold forms. In the words of the company's public-relations person, Vera's art continues to exude this same "aura of elegance."

Business grew; Vera headquarters moved from Manhattan to a shabby sandstone Georgian mansion on the Hudson River in Ossining, New York. The Neumanns lived on the second floor until they purchased a tract of land on top of a knoll overlooking the river, and a modernistic home—designed by architect-designer Marcel Breuer—was built; Breuer remained their friend throughout the years.

Vera decorated their house with the artistic efforts of Albers,

Vera Neumann and her husband with a model of Breuer-designed home

Vasarely, Picasso, Floris, Shahn, Calder, Noguchi—paintings, sculptures, drawings, mobiles, folk art, stabiles, animobiles, lithographs. Sitting in the living room overlooking the yard, a fifteen-foot Calder mobile moves in the breeze where the artist personally positioned it. Calder got in touch with Vera whenever he needed linens or bathroom towels.

The Neumanns designed the house in anticipation of children. But as the years went by and Vera did not become pregnant, the couple decided to travel to Europe—they were by that time too old to qualify to adopt American children—and bring home a family. They found a boy in Germany. The toddler had a Teutonic name and Vera suggested they rename him John. . . .

She was remembering her lover killed in the Spanish war, although she never told George. "He never asked. I felt if I named my child John it would be nice for me."

Several years later there was an addition to the family, a daughter, Evelyn. Vera was almost fifty, her husband four years older.

Vera is a believer in the extended-family concept. George's parents lived with them, simplifying her participation in the business with two small children at home. Before the children's arrival, the Neumanns shared chores. George shopped and often prepared Viennese dishes for the two of them; Vera did not enjoy cooking. The children were acquired when the parents were successful enough to hire household help, which, combined with the presence of Vera's in-laws, allowed her and her husband to travel and indulge in artistic interests. "He loved art, he loved music, he loved beautiful architecture," Vera remembers.

When Vera was fifty-four, her husband decided she needed a vacation. Her mother-in-law, Lona, whom she loved as a second mother, wished to visit Mexico. George persuaded his wife to make the trip with his mother over the Christmas holiday season while he stayed home with the children. She did so. Guilt lingers today as she remembers that her husband was on a mission for her when he had a fatal heart attack; he was driving to the airport to pick them up on their return. George Neumann was fifty-eight. His widow considers: "You know, I have wonderful memories and . . . I don't even feel sad about them, because I feel that George had obtained so many of the things he wanted to obtain while he was living. He saw the children grow and at the same time they were still little enough to be half decent [Vera laughs in her husky manner], and we traveled a lot. We did have grandparents at that time and it made it [easier]. . . . We knew they would be okay; it was a perfect setup." John was seven.

Evelyn was five. George's parents continued living in the flat-roofed glass Breuer house with their daughter-in-law.

Once, Vera considered remarriage. She says a psychiatrist convinced her to listen carefully to her children's thoughts on this move. Evelyn did not want her to wed; she tolerated the suitor only because "he used to bring her jellies," according to her mother. Today Vera says she has not really felt the lack of a man in her life. "Now whether that's true or false, I don't know. But I feel that I have not. Whether I will in a year or two when I'm really alone and I give up working. . . I think that it's. . ."

It is often puzzling to converse with Neumann; she constructs incomplete sentences, allowing others to add conclusions. Sometimes there is a syntax problem. Her hesitating speech gives the impression of unsureness. This is a false conclusion. She is forgetful. Her son-in-law—Evelyn's husband—remembers his humiliation when he first entered the family and Vera could not remember anyone's name. He now realizes, "She remembers things that nobody remembers, two hundred years ago, to the detail, and, you know, they are the important things. . . . She remembers art—oh, my God, does she!" Vera says she has been absent-minded all her life. She weeds out what she considers the nonessentials and concerns herself with what she believes to be important. If she is asked how many years ago John was adopted, her age when she met George, in what year her mother died, or the name of her long-employed housekeeper, acquaintances know she's likely to murmur, "I can't remember." In fact, she is not sure when she married George or the year of his death. She does remember her emotions, however.

George was not "tall, dark, and handsome"; he was pleasant-looking. "Of course I thought he was beautiful and I am sure he thought that I was very beautiful." He used to tell her just that.

There was no one better than Vera. He loved to take her to
designers in Vienna and buy her clothes, because "he wanted
beautiful surroundings." In Austria he insisted she buy "lace
dresses and all kinds of nonsense," she says. "I never really had
much reason for it." She reminisces and delights in the remembrances of his love. "We had so many things in common," says
Vera for perhaps the hundredth time.

Discussions of George continually arise and are held in almost
reverent tones. She tells how important his contributions were to
the ultimate success of Vera Industries. When pushed for a firm
statement on the relative roles they played, she suddenly shows
the toughness, straightforwardness, and logical thinking which is
somewhat blanketed by her elderly-aunt exterior persona, and
says, "I would have made it without him. Sure. I would have
made it." And she candidly and unexpectedly adds that *he*
couldn't have organized such a company without *her*, the artist,
the creator. Almost surprised at her admission, she qualifies:
"Everyone needs a George," and adds that men in business do not
succeed completely alone either. Everybody has help.

The tendency to give George credit is present among Vera's
associates as well, perhaps owing to respect for her feelings for
him. The president of Vera Industries requested that a tape recorder be stopped before he would comment on the relative influence each of the Neumanns had on the company's ultimate
prosperity.

Vera believes that only a man "who is not afraid of the wife
being dominant" will encourage his spouse's accomplishments.
Her press agent and friend, Rea Lubar, says that even if George
had never existed, ". . . there would have been a company and
Vera would have been the artist. . . . It was inevitable"; she was
destined to reach her present position. Vera's daughter feels it
would have taken her mother longer to become successful with-

out a supportive husband. Vera disagrees. George or no George, she'd be just where she is today.

A self-assured woman lies beneath the soft, accepting, faltering exterior. Although her son, daughter, and son-in-law playfully tease and humor their mother, when it comes down to decisions it is obvious the matriarch is listened to.

Vera's relationship with her now grown children is close. John dropped out of college, married "the wrong woman"—Vera protectively adds she was a "real crumb bum"—and is presently sculpting. Typically, Vera cannot remember the last name of the woman John Neumann has been living with for years ("Martha something"), but she knows she is fond of her—a Japanese-American, born in a "concentration camp in California or wherever they had those terrible things." Daughter Evelyn is married to the technical director of Vera Industries. (Vera playfully says, "He married into it!" and then she bursts into cackling laughter.) They live in what was Evelyn's and her brother's playhouse, an apartment-sized structure behind Vera's main house.

Proponents of the theory of alternation of generations will be delighted with the Neumanns. Evelyn—the product of an expensive boarding school—always wished her home was more in keeping with her friends' domiciles. Vera remembers her daughter wanting wall-to-wall carpeting in the bathroom—hardly the style for a Breuer house.

Growing up in the modernistic setting, Evelyn remembers her mother as strict "up to a point," and speaks of her "Jewish mother" aspect: making Ev wear galoshes when no one else did, as well as Danskin pants under dresses; not allowing her to attend co-ed parties, "and things like that." However, Evelyn remembers reaching a certain age, and all of a sudden her mother went "Whoop! The other way."

An example of Vera's new slant on the young-adult Evelyn was her feeling that the girl should not marry while in college. "My mother allowed herself to do this [when Vera lived with George] thirty-five years ago or forty, and I figured that she would allow me to do what she had done." Evelyn missed the point. It was not a case of Vera refusing to allow her daughter to cohabit; in fact, Vera would have preferred her to, in lieu of marriage. Evelyn won this particular difference of opinion and got married while she was in college. Yet she is still disappointed that she did not have her dream Plaza wedding and was wed instead on her mother's land overlooking a panoramic view of the Hudson, next to the Calder mobile. Ev: "I've always had plans and dreams about what I was going to do and where I was going to be, and a Plaza [Hotel] wedding was one that just didn't happen."

The artistic John shares his mother's interests and talents, although as a child he wondered about their wild, abstract paintings; they made him want to go to his room and close the door. Vera told her boy she liked them, and if he didn't she was sorry. She kept the artwork hanging on the walls, and it is still there.

Neumann most enjoys spending money on her now extensive art collection. From the beginning, her gifts and her husband's gifts to each other were works of art. Although they purchased the creations of artists who at the time were unknown, the Neumann collection is valuable today. "We bought them because we knew we were going to enjoy them forever. We didn't buy them because of the name. It now just so happens that it . . . it turns out to be . . . the most wonderful collection." She turns to an ink drawing of Robert Oppenheimer by Ben Shahn: "We bought this because we were fond of Oppenheimer." Two Calders—a sun and a giraffe in bright reds and blues—were a gift from George one Christmas. "Of course I was very fortunate to know Calder personally."

Vera recalls one day when the artist came to lunch and Evelyn was eating: "I have no idea what age she was; I don't remember at what age children are still in their highchairs." The little girl had a tic-tac-toe game consisting of a board with marbles. Calder was playing with Vera's youngster when one of the marbles rolled off the highchair tray onto the floor. The artist picked up a piece of Swiss cheese, slowly and methodically molded it into a sphere the size of a marble, and placed it in the tic-tac-toe game. Vera's eyes glisten as she remembers the delight on her daughter's face; she is equally pleased with this glimpse of Calder's personality, a man she felt deep affection for.

Vera's pleasure in being surrounded by fine art and folk designs carries over to her various showrooms throughout the country. These business centers are generally by Breuer, the designer of the popular cane-seated tubular Breuer chair. According to Vera President Tom Costello, "Going in, you're going to spend a lot of money whether you like it or not [when designing a showroom]. I say that in a very positive way, because whenever you work with him [Breuer] the investment is well worth it. So I wanted to do a shell [to save money] . . . and just sort of decorate the place, if you will. Vera said to me, 'Tom, let me tell you something. If you're gonna do a showroom, do it right or don't do it.' She gave me the courage to jump off the fence and spend a hell of a lot of dough. And I have to tell ya' . . . it has changed the whole nature of our home-furnishings division. Because what we always told people to do [display Vera merchandise in appropriate, attractive settings] . . . we did ourselves." Most clothing and textile merchandise showrooms are rather dingy affairs, poorly lit, with messy racks and shelves and with fabric thrown about. When one walks into Vera's, past the mounted scarves—which, when displayed hanging on a wall, become art—there is a feeling of lightness, space, and clean lines. Costello is right. The business headquarters of Vera Industries are unusual and special. These several showrooms—Costello refers to them as Taj Mahals—are in New York City.

Neumann spends her time at the Printex plant in Ossining. The original run-down mansion still forms the basis of the factory, with modern offices, studios, and manufacturing areas added to either side of the once-elegant sandstone structure. On the top floor, Neumann holds court in her studio where her dachshunds are kept from roaming by an expandable baby gate. Numerous Dundee marmalade jars filled with water for rinsing brushes (and for pouring into the canines' drinking bowl) sit on a snack table near the designer's drawing board. Folk art and a modern sofa grace the pleasant simple room. This is where she creates.

Her productions continue to be commercially successful. Her work for Burlington—designing bedsheets—is particularly outstanding, financially speaking. Yet it is difficult to imagine Neumann rubbing elbows in business with a Saint-Laurent, for example, who also has a bedding line. Actually she does not; Vera Neumann is on a different plane completely, with a retail domestic volume of twenty-eight million dollars. His is three hundred thousand dollars. Designers earn up to 5 percent of wholesale sales. When Fox Chapel and Sewickley, Pennsylvania, consumers were polled regarding familiarity with the world of fashion, color, and design, for a corporation interested in Vera Industries, less than 66 percent recognized the names Geoffrey Beene and Pierre Cardin. Out of eight designers, more people know Vera—82 percent—than any of the others. The little woman has a following. A Becker Research Corporation survey found that Vera was one of two designers shoppers recognized. Blass commented on the poll for the *New York Times:* "When you go west of the Hudson, designer recognition plummets."

What has kept Vera Neumann at the top of the textile-design

ladder for over thirty years against such competition as Pucci, Valentino, Pierre Cardin? Her young assistant plant manager, Tom Costick, espouses the public-relations spiel Vera employees have apparently memorized: "Vera *is* the Vera companies. . . . Vera with her husband, George Neumann, in 1966 traveled to Switzerland and purchased one of the first automatic silk-screening machines." If one has the patience to wait out the stock clichés, Costick does eventually say something substantive. Vera has an "innate" talent for developing a fine design which is technically manufacturable as well, he feels. This is unusual. She epitomizes the Bauhaus school of thought and incidentally is well versed in the theory: a compatible marriage is possible between technology and art; they do not necessarily work against each other. This post-World War I German philosophy compels the artist to train herself to be cognizant of the special problems of, for example, combining attractive colors for a summer scarf and at the same time producing a design which will show the silk-screening process at its best.

According to Costick, Neumann is unique among textile designers, for "most designers are not involved in the actual designing of the design," much less the technical aspects of the production. They purchase paintings from artists and add their signature. Period.

Neumann's ability to work within the Bauhaus philosophy—creating a well-designed, manufacturable, marketable product—sets her apart. One thing is clear: she is the chief artist at Vera Industries. Heavy words from Costick: "If anybody in the studio could keep up with Vera [she employs a stable of artists]—believe me, we'd have some hell of a country if we could all be like that."

The Vera people do respect Neumann's talents and productiveness. They say—and she concurs—that she designs enough scarf patterns within a year to result in three hundred and sixty

Canines and Neumann under Oppenheimer portrait and her father-in-law's "Sunflowers"

Vera, wearing Calder pin, at work in her Ossining studio

marketed pieces, many in several color combinations. If everyone is exaggerating and she actually produces half of what they claim, this from an almost seventy-year-old commercial designer—indeed, from an artist of any age—is amazing. Vera comments: "People say, 'How can you create hundreds of designs a year?' That's easy!" Costello says, "That's her joy. I sit having a cup of coffee with Vera and she's painting with one hand, talking with me, and answering the telephone with the other. Oh, hell, yes." She also manages to squeeze in interviews, directors' meetings, staff conferences, board consultations, and inspirational travels, the last resulting in, for example, "Painted Boats," an Oriental design after a China trip.

It is interesting that although the Vera employees consider her work "art," she calls it commercial design. The differentiation lies in her Bauhaus leanings. To be true to this philosophy, she cannot simply paint for art's sake. Would she like to be purely an artist, with no business connection? A quick answer, "Yes." She considers: "I don't feel that I am painting the things I would like to paint if I were a painter. But I don't know whether I have much time left." She chuckles deeply. She would most enjoy creating "very abstract" art but wonders if "they are commercial enough or not," and adds that she is typed, as an actress would be, to create a certain sort of nonabstract pattern. The "Vera look."

Neumann's effect on all aspects of the Vera Industries is great. Yet it is hard to transcend the initial impression of this corporate scion as a loving, somewhat dippy, scatterbrained aunt who could not possibly be interested in anything more profound than her planned menu for dinner that day. Probably these facets of the woman are actually present. But there is another whole area which must surprise everyone who comes in contact with her. For she seesaws between the two worlds. On how she would like to be remembered: ". . . as a well-rounded person and a good mother, as good as I could possibly be . . . or expect to be and . . . a . . . and I think I would like to be known as a human . . . hum . . . humane person, and I think I am sensitive to people, and that counts more to me than what . . . how much the person has or what the person looks like. . . ."

Tom Costello on Neumann: "Oh, yes, she knows herself pretty well. She's aware of all her abilities. . . . She is the taste arbiter of the company . . . instinctive, great taste. I happen to like her a lot, but I also have a lot of respect for her and I work very closely with her. She is one of the most direct, honest-spoken people you'll meet. She's willing to risk the relationship to say what's in her head. Absolutely."

She is physically demonstrative. If she feels affectionate toward someone, even an interviewer, she will hug and kiss goodbye. It would be hard to dislike Vera Neumann, an unassuming, straightforward individual. It is also hard to imagine her angry. Costello says, "She gets mad at stupidity. Incompetence. She will tolerate incompetence, in my opinion, if it is not under a smoke screen . . . she's able to blow *that* away immediately. There are people who are only fair at what they do, but are honest about it. I think Vera has a tendency to allow that, realizing that everyone is not great. Sham, Vera won't put up with. Artistic infringement makes her very angry. And rightly so, because she's better than anyone else." Neumann has a temper. Costello says, "She can give a shave and a haircut" with the best of them. Her public-relations person says that in a disagreement Neumann has the last word. Costello: "Many times, I have to tell ya', she doesn't agree with what's being done from a personal standpoint, but she's objective enough from a business standpoint to realize there is what I call commercial aesthetics."

At business conferences Neumann often sits back, hesitates, thinks. Then, says a Vera executive, "She drops a one-liner. She's phenomenal." Everyone—including Neumann—agrees she hates board meetings. They are not her thing; she's very uncomfortable with them. On the other hand, someone will ask a question, and, in the words of a colleague, "Here are all these great businessmen and Vera will answer that question in her own little manner, and her response is exactly, precisely to what the person asked."

The power of the woman, her viewpoints and liberal leanings, are evident throughout the corporation. At the Vera companies one sees women in upper executive positions; the merchandising vice-president (scarf division) and the executive vice-president (linens division) are both females in their early thirties. They are essentially in charge of those two sections. Neumann believes success comes to a woman "with the times, the opportunity, the chance that one has, also the surroundings she comes from. I think you need a little bit of something more for a woman." She remembers Mrs. Albans, who used to visit her mother when Vera was a child. Mrs. Albans wrote poetry and her sister decorated the pages with roses. But, says Neumann, "You never got out of the tea parties" then if you were a woman artist.

Neumann did "get out of the tea parties." Manhattan and Vera executives consider her a valuable commodity. What will happen when Neumann, as she says it, "kicks"? She frankly suggests that maybe it will all fall apart without her.

It is difficult to imagine this show forging ahead deprived of its creative and spiritual force. The entire organization mirrors Vera's taste and style as she, for example, mixes Papa Neumann paintings—those of her late father-in-law—with Calders on the showroom walls.

Vera loves music as well as art—"I'm a jazz nut"—and enjoys baroque and Bach. Her pleasures are simple. She reads in the art field—Matisse's biography is a favorite—and likes autobiographies and volumes on various countries. She has read a great deal about Oppenheimer and Martin Luther King.

On a certain level Neumann lacks sophistication, pretensions. Her presence among the beautiful people of the designing industry is curious. As it turns out, she's the high priestess of them all. The woman designs bedspreads, draperies, tablecloths, place mats, napkins, sheets, towels, napkin rings, scarves, stoneware, china, women's sportwear, needlepoint, fabrics, wallpaper, umbrellas, lingerie.

Perry Ellis, Vera designer—with a sculptured, aristocratic head and high cheekbones, attired in casual chic—speaks of his boss in his genteel Virginia tones: "She tells wonderful stories, she loves to laugh. I meet a lot of people in varying degrees of success in the course of a week. Sometimes this makes people forget where they came from and places them on an unreal plane in their relationships to others. But Vera is a very consistent person. There is an earthy quality to her and I don't mean that as men speak of voluptuousness, referring to breasts. It's not that at all. I mean 'earth' as a quality which is natural and real."

Question: Is there anything about her that bothers you?

Answer: "You know, I wish there were. . . ."

This is the woman who, when told in confidence by a doctor that her Scottish housekeeper had terminal cancer, got in touch with the woman's priest in Edinburgh. Neumann directed him to concoct a letter calling the ill woman back to Scotland; through Vera's maneuvering, the Scots lady died at home with her family. "She was so Catholic . . . I felt it would mean a great deal to her to be surrounded by her loved ones."

Vera Neumann is an odd mixture. At times it is hard to believe—although Vera doesn't seem to have any trouble accepting it—that this five-foot Jewish daughter of Russian immigrants has risen to the top of her field in the United States. What you do think of when you meet her is how much she reminds you of your Aunt Rose.

2

SYNERGY AND SWIMSUITS

Gillian Mitchell and Jacqueline Baird

————————•⊷∞⊷•————————

> Syn • er • gism: The simultaneous action of
> separate agencies which, together, have greater
> total effect than the sum of their individual
> effects.
> *–Harper Dictionary of Modern Thought*

THE TWINS WERE BORN in a British seaside town; today these
millionaire bikini-manufacturing partners consider Florida their
permanent home. "I wouldn't want to live anywhere else, mind
you, but in America," says older twin, Jacqueline, and Gillian
adds, "Oddly enough, it [southeastern Florida] is the nicest place
in the world."

They should know. A duo in an international act from their
sixteenth year, these identical twins—born in 1931—lived in a
dozen countries as entertainers. Their story, however, begins in
Hove, next to Brighton, on the southern coast of England.

Gillian, nicknamed Gill (pronounced as if spelled with a "J"),
remembers their father was absent during their childhood. The

black sheep of his family, he joined England's merchant marine at fourteen and eventually became a wartime commander in the Navy. After having been at sea for months, when Charles Davis was home his relationship with his wife, Madeline, was strained. They slept in separate rooms. Jackie says there was no physical warmth. "No," agrees Gill. "Yet we didn't realize until we were twelve that they were not really happy." During the twins' twelfth year, the Davises divorced; the separation did not change the girls' close feeling or contact with their father. Calling them Jac and Gill, he still stayed in their home each spring for three weeks, and, Jackie recalls, "We had a tremendous affection for our father. . . . I mean, very, very strong, even though we did not see him often. Probably we only saw him at his best, you see. . . . Mind you, for us it wasn't traumatic because everyone else's father was away, as well, at war. . . . There was no 'Oh, dear, isn't it dreadful, we don't have a daddy at home.'"

Both Jacqueline and Gillian believe it was hardest for Madeline Davis, a young worrying mother. German bombers regularly flew over Hove on their way to London, and "On the way back, if they had been chased off by Spitfires, of course they would give us a little token of their esteem," remembers Jackie. At the time, there was little transportation and the children tied this woman down; her life was dominated by empty days and nights, as the three lived in a section of a large house, renting the remainder. Jacqueline says her mother probably thought, If only I didn't have the children. "I don't know what went on in her mind," says Gillian.

Thirty-five when her twin daughters were born, she had, according to her sister, a persecution complex from a young age. "It's not fair. I'm being put down," Madeline often complained. As an adult, she had no contact with her family. The only warm

feeling she exhibited was for her dead father, whom she re-
minisced about frequently.

Although she spoke of her father, Mrs. Davis, a petite woman
with short auburn hair and a fine figure (Gillian says she "worked
on it"), was not sentimental. A positive thinker, organized but
rather untidy, their mother, Jacqueline says, was the "most un-
easygoing person in the world." Gillian describes her as "hyper."

Not a typical British "mum," Madeline Davis was a well-read
student of various religions—she considered Buddhism to be the
most intellectual and Judaism the most logical—and a vegetar-
ian. A strict one. "Oh, what a bore," comments Gill. Although
meat was forbidden in their house, Mrs. Davis considered fish
acceptable. According to Jackie, her mother explained that sea-
food has no feelings. Rather before her time in this respect, she
was perhaps reactionary in the matter of discipline.

The girls were in a dance recital at the age of three, and a
three-foot whip, plaited, with an inch-long leather thong at the
end was a prop. Madeline Davis put it to practical use. According
to her children, when they made her angry she hit "all the way
down the back, and down the back of the neck." Jackie's voice
becomes almost meek while Gill claims it didn't bother them.
"Yes, it does mar you, Gillian," says Jackie. "You never lose that
resentment. Never... You really don't." In addition to whip-
pings, Mrs. Davis believed in spankings. "Yes," says Jackie. "And
some," adds Gill. Jackie: "I felt rather cowed by her."

Their home life was not affectionate; "We had no younger
brothers or sisters... we had nothing maternal at all.... There
was no physical warmth," remembers Jackie. "No," confirms
Gillian. "Kissing Mother was like shaking hands, in a way, after a
long absence.... We never felt we wanted to sit on Mother's
knee." Jackie wishes her parent had been more of a mother.

Gillian doesn't think it hurt her: "I thought she was super! Very forceful. Gave you total independence." She finds it difficult to articulate her feelings further.

Anyway, both twins remark, they had each other. When Mrs. Davis was angry at one of her daughters, they teamed up and spoke softly in front of their parent, who, being hard of hearing, became furious that they were whispering about her.

The woman was ill. When Jacqueline and Gillian were thirteen, Mrs. Davis had a complete mental breakdown. "It wasn't too bad until we went to the hospital and she didn't even know who we were," says Gillian, who had a "dreadful lost feeling." Their mother's arguments with relatives were particularly unfortunate at this time; there was no one to turn to. Charles Davis was at sea. They lived at home alone for weeks, purchasing groceries with a food-coupon book until their mother recovered. Today they feel this reinforced their sense of independence and the ability to care for themselves.

After her recovery, Madeline Davis decided to remove her girls from their private day school and enroll them in a boarding school in the next town. "We didn't like it particularly but it was good not to be under the roof so much. . . ." They sneaked home twice a week to have a meal with their mother. After one year they returned to Wistons, their day school, until graduation.

Before they graduated, their mother had sold the family house and tried several unsuccessful ventures. Charles Davis, skippering pleasure yachts in the Mediterranean after the war, lived a nice life but with little pay. Since aid was not forthcoming from either parent, the twins realized they must build their own financial success. So after high school they "went straight into show business," Jackie remembers. Had they always wanted to do that? "No contest!" states Gill.

The Davis sisters began their adult lives with a sense of adventure and, through circumstances, an independent and self-sufficient outlook. And with the help of the process of synergism they gained a greater total strength together than each possessed alone. One plus one equaled three.

These sisters disagree with the often touted idea of separating twins; Gillian points out, "You don't do that with brothers and sisters." Both admit to loving the attention they attract, and feel they carry an extra identity rather than the other way around. Jacqueline: "We've always made the most of it." Her hair is the identical color and style of her sister's and they are the same size. Until one knows them better and recognizes slight differences, they appear to be doubles. They always were—and continue to be—best friends. When their mother told them, "You're not leaving the house one at a time, you know. If you want to go out on the road, you're going to be together," they agreed, and left home at the age of sixteen.

There were no acting parts for twins and one had to be tall for the chorus line; the sisters are five feet three. So they became a dance team and auditioned for acts in London where, almost miraculously, they were hired immediately by a troupe. As members of a six-girl group, a show-business odyssey began, lasting seventeen years, until they were thirty-four.

"It was a good act. . . . We knew this was not for the future, but it was wonderful for then. . . . Ballet, modern stuff, tap . . . we finished with an acrobatic closing that absolutely brought the house down. Flying splits and walking on our hands and swinging each other around and . . ."

Gillian: "I can still walk on my hands!"

Jacqueline: "I couldn't do a *split* if you paid me a *million* dollars." Spoken with a properly indignant English mannerism.

Having gained experience performing with the group, they decided to organize their own act. Although their last name was

Davis, they chose to tour under the name The Hamilton Twins. According to the sisters, Davis has a masculine connotation in the United Kingdom; Lady Hamilton, on the other hand, is a well-known name in English history.

Their mother loaned them cash to start their act. When they originally left Hove, she insisted an amount of money be sent home every week. Her daughters say she was a person who "poor-mouthed." She was tight-fisted with a pound. "Very. Very," states Gillian. "Oh, yes. Every dime." Years later, they discovered that Mrs. Davis had placed their funds in a bank account in their name. Asked if they could have used the money at the time, Gillian said, "Ohhh, we *desperately* needed it, yes." Jacqueline, less emphatic: "Ah, there were very few times we *desperately* needed it. [Jacqueline often moderates her sister's comments as Gillian listens and accepts her doing so.] By the time we got it, we didn't need it of course."

Money became less important as their act proved financially and professionally successful. Together they toured the world.

Their eyes light up as they recall those years and Gillian says, "We love our past. We did *all* the things we wanted to do . . . including the show-business side of it, which wasn't a *huge* element in our lives. But seeing the world *was!* I remember someone saying, 'You must make it in New York City now you're here, and you've got to knock on doors.' *What?* Knock on doors and sit in those horrid little offices? No way!" Gillian tends to speak in italics and exclamation points. Not overly serious about the professional aspects of show business, they continued mainly because it afforded them a traveling life-style. "Whatever a youngster can do and see in the world will make him a richer person," says Gillian.

Their personal lives as they toured were full of new experiences. Gillian remembers falling in love with an American in

Switzerland. "I flipped my cork, yes. He said, 'How do you do?'
and my knees buckled. I never want to go through *that* experience again!" Gillian and her lover were intimate for about a year
and traveled together throughout Europe. Her sister remembers
the couple left her in Geneva for three weeks, and, she says, "I
nearly went bonkers."

Question: Why didn't you take Jacqueline along?

Gillian: "Oh, very funny."

Jacqueline: "Friendly we were but not *that* friendly." Eventually Gillian tired of her American.

Jacqueline first fell in love in Pakistan with a Swiss, she says
dreamily, softly. "But it isn't a very good memory." They became
engaged and corresponded for a year but seemed to grow apart
except on paper. "George Veeland was a very nice chap; I felt
dreadful when I decided that I wished to end the arrangement."
Love affairs continued to occur between their travels.

They performed in Cairo before they were twenty-one.
Whenever they arrived on the Continent for a booking, they gave
their names to an agent who set up future engagements. They
had connections in Italy and France. The Hamilton Twins
toured Hungary, Puerto Rico, Panama, Spain.

"San Salvador, Peru—Name it, we've gone!" bubbles Gillian.
"Everyone loves New York and everyone wants to make it, I
suppose, and do well, but we did the Hilton Hotel tour, my
goodness!" Two months of performing in night clubs within the
Hilton chain around the world left their days free to enjoy the
local surroundings. They swam at the British Country Club in
Calcutta. Gillian loved it. So did Jacqueline after she managed to
get over the "dreadful poverty."

Life was a fling for them; they signed to perform only where
they wished to visit. "Obviously you are going to go skiing. Why
else would you get a contract in Switzerland? There would be no

The Hamilton Twins on stage

point!" says Gillian. There were logistical problems, however, because they had no home base. When traveling to perform in a skiing country, they were in a panic to retrieve equipment left in another part of the world. "We could do a tour of the world collecting clothes"; out-of-season frocks were left with various friends and acquaintances. Items were lost. It was a frantic, nonstop kind of existence. Their eyes glow as they recount it. On to France!

Their father, Commander Davis, was living on the French Riviera in Nice, near Cannes. While their mother never discouraged their ambition to enter show business, Charles Davis felt differently. From a solid British background—although a black sheep himself—he was shocked that they were going on the stage. He discouraged them but, according to his daughters, not in an unkind way. "It was a social thing with him." Not proper. Four years after the girls formed their own act, they got a contract to play the Cannes Casino, billed as "Le Hamilton Twins." The Commander drove to Cannes to see his daughters perform. His reaction: "I used to be known as Commander Davis. Now I'm just known as the father of the twins!" According to them, he was delighted with their success. Jacqueline remembers her father as being "really good-looking"; Gillian describes him as "gorgeous." They both loved to have him pick them up when they were schoolgirls, for all their friends "swooned over that good-looking man."

During their show-business years, they were organized, methodical, businesslike. "Mummie used to say, 'A business letter typed has far more impact,'" remembers Gillian. They traveled with their Olivetti, typing professional letters to agents. Quite unusual for a road act to present such a classy aura.

With time and experience, the act improved. When the sisters were in their early twenties, it consisted mainly of acrobatics,

singing, and dancing. They "put a song over," but did not consider themselves vocalists. With success, The Hamilton Twins
found it less burdensome to continue to send a check home to
Madeline Davis.

Throughout their traveling years, their mother had a variety of
mental disorders. When her letters began to get longer and
longer, and every detail in her life was discussed, trouble was
brewing. In 1954, when they were entertaining in Spain, Mrs.
Davis came to visit them. The trip ended with Jacqueline having
to fly back to England with her mother and deliver her to a
mental institution. "That was a horrible experience, it really
was." Jacqueline Davis recalls her parent logically and knowl-
edgeably discussing the need for a nonigniting fuel with a stew-
ardess during the flight. Her daughter had trouble drawing a line
between "what's sane and what's not." Then Mrs. Davis began
her "your sister's evil" type of conversation. "I had to take her. . . .
It was awful," remembers Jacqueline. Her mother was hospitalized for several months.

Although Madeline Davis—who had four severe mental
episodes—was not an affectionate person, the twins today feel
they are warm and loving—although not demonstrative—toward
each other. Their show-business career helped to further a sense
of independence and self-worth and taught them how to be physically warm to others, as most performers are, after a childhood
with a mother who lacked this capability.

Their mother was sixty-four when she died in 1959. Her
daughters, twenty-eight years old, were in Venezuela working for
a television producing company when they received a telephone
call relating, in broken English, the essence of a telegram. They
asked the director as he started to offer condolences not to say
another word to anyone, or to them. The filming was completed

with controlled emotions; discretion in public is easiest for everyone, they believe.

Fifteen minutes "do make a difference," according to Gillian. Jackie, born a quarter of an hour earlier than her sister, flew home and took the responsibility of burying their mother; cash was not available for both to make the trip.

With their mother's death, desire for a permanent home began to grow. After performing in Miami on several occasions, they decided to rent an apartment; finally there was a place to leave out-of-season garments. They continued to travel, for it was impossible to find enough work to survive in Florida during the warmer months.

The performers had had other clothes-related problems occasionally. Once while they were touring, costumes were stolen; they quickly made new ones. They were never taught to be seamstresses during their childhood, but, according to Gillian, "Show business makes you sew," for outfit alterations and repairing are frequent. A Singer sewing machine traveled with them. They remember setting it on airport seats, hoping it would be there when they returned after checking their luggage. Overseas baggage rates were expensive and sewing machines heavy, so they surreptitiously hand-carried it aboard.

In addition to designing and mending costumes as they traveled, they began to sew bikinis. Where it was bad form to wear skimpy attire, they wore matching pleated miniskirts.

In the fifties, bikinis were forbidden on some parts of the American seashore. After a winter working and sunbathing in Mexico, they found themselves that summer in New Jersey where a lifeguard ordered them off the beach. "'You have to cover up. You can't wear that,' he said. I thought he was joking. I couldn't believe him! *He* couldn't believe *me!*" states Jacqueline.

They find this whole episode amusing; French women had been wearing bikinis for thirty years. Gillian says, "We couldn't understand the morality of it. When you [Americans] are so almost puritan in your outlook and so modern in your life, it's a great contrast. It's a paradox. I thought, Oh my, they're so modern in their plumbing; why are they so unmodern in their brains?"

Outside the United States, bikinis were acceptable and Jacqueline and Gillian Davis liked working in warm climates where bathing suits were practically the daily uniform. They continued to sew their own bathing suits. At the Panama Hilton, Jacqueline says, "The little stewardesses couldn't get over" the twin's bathing suits; they wanted the same bikinis the twins wore. The sisters made them suits. Gillian says: "A friend of ours who was running the pool—an Australian girl with whom we are still friendly —said to us, 'Wise up, girls, you don't *give* them away. You *sell* them and augment your salary!'"

The first week they actually marketed the suits—they were in the Dominican Republic at the time—they made a profit of over a hundred dollars. "We were selling bikinis right, left, and center," remembers Gillian. The year was 1963, just when the bikini craze began, and it was finally acceptable in most parts of the United States to wear a skimpy swimsuit. Their timing was perfect.

Once again they traveled to Puerto Rico and performed at the Caribe Hilton, the Americana, and the Condado Beach Hotel. Working in their room or sunning by the Condado pool, they hand-sewed hooks and eyes, and completed other necessary handwork. "If you've got nothing to do, it beats boredom. You can't be 'doing' all the time," states Jacqueline. Gillian adds, "You can't sit around a pool all day . . . and maybe play an hour's tennis." And she qualifies, "Of course, in the evening we had the show to do."

Materials and supplies scattered around them by poolside were a subtle advertisement. "We put the price up [on a sign] at one point and sold double," relates Jacqueline, who adds with delight, "Can you believe that? It got to the point where it was ridiculous."

The suits were placed in the hotel's Mermaid Shop on consignment.

Back in Miami where they had their apartment, a friend introduced them to a man in the garment business who allowed them to purchase end cuts of fabric. A Cuban woman named Isolina Hernández—a seamstress—began sewing for them in the evenings after her regular job.

Orders from stores began pouring in. The twins would simply walk into a shop, ask to see the person in charge, and the suits, according to them, sold themselves. When they approached a Florida specialty store, Swim 'n' Sport, they received an order for three dozen. "How can we ever make three dozen suits by next week?" Gillian and Jacqueline said to each other. They managed. Hernández hired her sister, the girl down the street, and another neighbor. Eventually an army of women was making bikinis.

Both sun worshipers, the Davises were sick of Buffalo, New York, Boston, and Pittsburgh in the winter. "We fell in love with Miami," says Gillian. Since the entertainment business is seasonal in Miami, they thought they might be able to combine the two—show business and sewing—and live permanently in Florida.

A tennis partner of theirs—Barney Boardman, from Augusta, Georgia—occasionally ordered suits for his girl friends. Eventually, the three tennis players each put up a few thousand dollars and opened a shop. Gillian describes him as "the most unlikely human to be in the garment business in the whole wide world . . .

about as unlikely as two limey ladies—*shiksas* as well!"

Isolina Hernández, her sister, and her neighbors sewed for the twins in their homes for over five years. Born in Havana and a Miamian since 1956, Hernández recalls, in her heavy Cuban accent, Gillian or Jacqueline pleading with her ("I don't know what is Jackie and what is Gill, you know? At that time.") to work for them: "One day she was in my house. 'Iso, we find the people have the money for do the business. Oh, Iso, I like-a how you make it. Please help me, I *need* you. . . . I need your work. Don't be afraid now [to quit your secure job], Iso: *I need you.*'" All the principals connected with the venture were single: the twins, Boardman, Hernández's sister, and Isolina Hernández, who says, "You know something? When we start that business, it's a real family. I put complete my heart in that business."

Gillian recalls Hernández saying, "I'll work for you in the shop as long as I don't have to work for any man and it's just the two of you who are going to be there." Barney Boardman was rarely in the rented store/factory, which they named the Bikini Shop, on Miami Beach. The front was the retail section; manufacturing and shipping areas were in the rear.

Neither of the twins liked the direct-customer aspect of the business. Jacqueline truly hated it. An artistic individual, she stuck to designing. "I'd get busy and think, We'll have it that color, and just at that point a customer would interrupt. Oh, rats!"

Gillian describes the huge table in the back of the shop where Isolina had a rather primitive cutting machine; Gillian constantly worried that she would lose a finger. Hernandez still has ten.

There was a shipping problem; the table used for cutting was also the shipping platform. Isolina sewed by day, left at six o'clock, and the twins had an hour before rushing off to rehearsals as, during this initial business period, they continued to perform. One drove home to get costumes, ran back to the shop to pick up the other, and then both headed for the night club. After the show, back to the shop at eleven o'clock. This was the only time they could use the cutting-shipping table to package their goods.

The lights automatically went off in the shop at 3 A.M. On several occasions they thought the electricity had failed, only to realize they were still working in the middle of the night. "It was too tough," says Jackie. They received no salary for the first six months.

An offer to perform at a prestigious club in Monte Carlo took them abroad again. "You can't run a factory and go off for three months!" friends said to them. But they did. In addition, they played Cannes and Nice, then flew back to oversee their business once again. While they were gone, their pattern-maker, forelady, and general right-hand woman, Isolina Hernández, coped with sixty signed blank checks and a ten-thousand-dollar bank balance.

"I think at that time too much for me, you know? I be afraid." Not familiar with the intricacies of manufacturing, Hernández bought material—those first suits were all gingham checks—at Grant's or Kress's at retail prices. The twins sent trim from France.

They returned, organized the window displays, ironed, carried out garbage. . . . Hernández referred to them—and still does— collectively as "she." Example: "She very very smart."

Question: Who?

Answer: Jackie and Gill.

The corporate name was The Twins, Inc. Their logo: two mermaids with long blond hair facing each other with their tails swinging out, one to the left, the other to the right.

For errands, the hard-working sisters used to borrow the "wretched non-air-conditioned car of Allen's, right?" Gillian says

Iran Issa-Khan

Gillian and Jacqueline in their polar bear print

to Jacqueline. Jackie describes their friend's auto as an old Buick, "with holes in the side, called Duchess. . . . A monster." And they delivered the merchandise to the retail outlets in Allen's car. There was constant confusion regarding street numbers. Gillian would go to Thirty-seventh Street and find she was supposed to be at Thirty-seventh *Avenue*, forty-five minutes across town—a difficult mistake to make in Miami's simplistic checkerboard street layout. The twins were overworked.

Sales figures rose. During this phase of business growth, Gillian Davis fell in love with Earl Mitchell, an ex-F.B.I. agent and ex-police chief. "I was never going to get married. Period," states Gillian. Today—a decade after her wedding at thirty-six—she says it is "the greatest life. I'm a lucky girl." Jacqueline says of her sister's husband, now a realtor, "He is so super."

The increased activity generated by rising volume crowded the Bikini Shop; factory space was rented in an industrialized area in northwest Dade County. After the wedding, between policework and exam-taking for his real-estate license, Gillian's new husband worked for the twins as a carpenter in the new facility, building bars off the floor—"air space"—for garments on hangers. "It's not a good idea, is it, Gill? For a husband to work for a wife?" queries Jacqueline. "He should do his thing and I should do my thing," states Gillian Davis Mitchell emphatically.

Although the Davises decided they would never marry, in the end both did. Jacqueline met her husband-to-be while working at the Panama Hilton. She accompanied friends to a golf course, although she argued that she didn't care for the game. The winner of the tournament was a pro golfer, Butch Baird. Baird, a divorced man, and Jacqueline Davis married two years after Gillian and Earl.

Work at Mrs. Baird's and Mrs. Mitchell's manufacturing plant escalated. The at-home Cuban seamstresses began working at the factory in Hialeah. Six or seven of them drove together. Although Gillian thought their new facility was huge, within a year it, too, was cramped. Additional space was rented a block away. The two women ran—with Isolina—between the buildings until, in 1976, one 5,000-square-foot air-conditioned area was rented. Today they are again searching for more footage.

As the business grew, so did Jacqueline Davis Baird's family. In 1969, she became pregnant. After the Caesarean delivery—"I'm too tiny"—of her daughter Julie, The Hamilton Twins did two shows, the only performances Butch Baird ever saw. Jacqueline turns to her sister: "Gilly, we had to work for weeks going to jazz class to get back into shape." Gillian agrees. "All those acrobatics, leaps in the air, and flying splits we did! Our act was so so *crazy!*" They gave up show business after those performances; it was too physically strenuous to perform only periodically. Said Jacqueline, "It was impossible. The next day you couldn't do your shoe up."

Jacqueline had a second child, Michael, nicknamed "Briney" after a literary character. In 1973, she saw a television program, then an article, about abandoned Oriental children. The result of this was the adoption of a Korean orphan, Yanine, obtained through an Oregon agency. Jackie and Butch Baird employ a Honduran girl to care for the children. Jacqueline does not allow the South American women to speak English. She wishes the children to learn Spanish, and feels that, although it is selfish not to permit her housekeeper to learn the language surrounding her, it is more important that her youngsters have a second language.

Gillian Mitchell has no children. Her husband, Earl, was married three times before wedding Gill. Father of several children, he is unable to have a child with his fourth wife, owing to surgery. Earl Mitchell—soft-spoken graduate of the University of Indiana, ex-miler (4.8 minutes in 1941)—comments: "When Jackie got pregnant, she [Gillian] was as jealous as she could be. . . . No way in the world she wanted to be left out. Prior to that, she hadn't cared one way or the other. And all of a sudden she realized how happy Jackie was . . . and then she wanted one [a baby] too. It wore off in a hurry . . . disappeared almost as fast as it came up. And now she's absolutely delighted to have no children."

Jacqueline says of her sister: "I think it was the idea of my doing something she couldn't do. You know when you're a twin . . . Go back to that basic thing that you always do the same thing. . . . She was very upset when I got pregnant, because she knew that she couldn't."

Jacqueline Baird's life—with three children and a business—is full. Gillian Mitchell says she misses the limelight of show business; Jacqueline feels her husband as a pro golfer has the stardom in her family, and has no desire for the attention. They both are models once a year, however.

The women perceived a unique catalogue idea where all models are sets of twins. They include themselves, in their mid-forties, in bikinis. Both look terrific. Jacqueline, after two Caesareans, has somehow maintained a flawless tummy for publication. Five feet three and trim size sevens, they weigh about 107. If a bathing suit does not fit them properly, in their opinion something is wrong; in their company's bikini, they wear a "small." Being the same size is a convenience. When a winter coat was needed for buying trips North, the cost was shared, as they are never absent from the business at the same time. Pairs of boots are worn by both (they wear the same shoe size). Physical doubles.

One of the few chances to tell Jac from Gill is when they talk. Gillian, the peppier, exuberant half of the set, has a sharp, nasal, urgent manner of speech. Speaking rapidly—in staccato—she likes to affect a playful cockney accent, sprinkling her conversation with "luv" and "ducky." Jacqueline also inserts a rare "luv" here and there; she sometimes says "my dear" or "lovey," as well, in proper British tones, but tends to be a more cautious, less effervescent, yet still effusive conversationalist, exuding warmth. She has a gentle smile and creases beneath her eyes, and speaks in a low, sultry tone; Jacqueline seems a softer, milder individual. Strangely, her deep voice is not readily apparent when one is conversing face-to-face with her. Perhaps her general femininity blocks the reality of the Tallulah Bankhead tones. She is subtle, pleasant. Jacqueline uses the first names of others a great deal in conversation, giving a personal tone to her speech patterns. Both women are outgoing, and vivacious conversationalists.

Isolina Hernández says they speak excellent Spanish in the

factory. Both are fluent in French, and converse in Italian as
well. Gillian is teaching herself German, using a tape recorder in
her car. Where did they learn Spanish, for example? "Why, in
Spain!" bubbles Gill.

Their Spanish-speaking Cuban workers are almost all female.
Gillian, blond head cocked to one side, considering for the
first time, says, "That's funny, isn't it?" The head of the shipping department is a female; all the shipping department employees are women except Jerry, their "fetcher and carrier."
Gillian Mitchell hates "to even venture to say they do work
better." Jackie Baird flatly states females are better employees:
"We've never had a problem with women. We've had [male]
cutters come and go. . . . We've had problems with the men. . . ."

A closely knit group works for the twin bosses. Of Isolina
Hernández's original twelve seamstresses in 1962, eleven are still
employed by The Twins, Inc. Their bookkeeper for nine years
comments on male bosses versus female: "There's a friendlier
feeling; it's different. . . working for women."

One man holds a responsible position within the corporation.
Barney Boardman, the twins' partner, oversees budgets, bank
loans, and financing while the two women handle design, manufacturing, and merchandising. "We never tell him how to run
the office and he never tells us how to design a bikini," says
Jacqueline. "Which is super. We work many hours longer, of
course." While the sisters labor closely together, Boardman
comes in in the late afternoon for a short time—they say he takes
worry home while they lock the door and forget—with really no
idea what the twins' work entails. They wish he appreciated them
more. They know what *he* does. . . . "He thinks you can cut a
square, just like that [Gillian holds up a 4″ × 4″ piece of polyester
fabric], and that's a bra"—they both laugh—"because the fabric's
stretchy! It's frustrating, in a way, that your own partner doesn't

know what you do. . . . He hasn't a clue." They were born under the sign of Gemini—"the Twins"—and Boardman gave his partners Gemini necklaces with little gold twins on them. "If we ever had a second line, we would call it 'Gemini, a subsidiary of The Twins, Inc.,'" says Jacqueline Baird. Both feel strongly about astrology. Baird: "I think it's absolute hogwash." Gillian: "Isn't it for people who have nothing else to do?" They have plenty to do. When asked if they will ever retire, they both look aghast. "What would you ever do?" questions Jacqueline Baird.

These Gemini twins view their rapidly expanding company as a creative corporation and like to think of themselves as ". . . the girls who started this fun company. Pretty things . . . colorful, summery . . . are more fun than uniforms. When you think of The Twins, you should think, Thank God summer is here! Let's make the person from Buffalo who lies on the beach in a pretty suit, let's make her happy! We love that sort of thing! . . . Oh, yes, we're two girls—twins—who started this great bikini company; we almost pioneered in bikinis. You couldn't *get* a bikini here when we first started. Our timing was really lucky."

Timing, organization, drive, and a tremendous amount of energy . . . The soft chatter of Spanish-speaking voices fills the air-conditioned interior of The Twins, Inc., which is housed in a bright green building. The company phone is answered, "Twins," and office staffers refer to their bosses as "the twins." Gillian Mitchell's desk—as she oversees manufacturing—is in the general office area; Jacqueline Baird's private office is a somewhat disorganized affair. Hanging on her wall is a framed needlework stating, "I'm too busy to be organized." Behind Jackie Baird's metal desk are photos of The Hamilton Twins from show-business days, and of her children, including an engaging photograph of Briney playing golf in the shadow of his dad, Butch Baird, also swinging a club.

The concrete building in this light-industrial area—with about a hundred and fifty employees—is busy with the sounds of sewing machines, buttonholers, cutting machinery. Isolina Hernández runs the shop. "I say, 'This is my son grow up,' you know?" Hernández today owns two duplexes and two houses. The Twins, Inc., pays her a bonus of 5 percent of profits.

Hernández is pleased; profits are rising.

The corporation's line includes hats, cover-ups, jump suits, one-piece bathing suits, bikinis, skirts, and shirts—according to Gill Mitchell, "everything you want to go for a weekend in Nassau with." The merchandise is handled by stores such as Lord & Taylor, Bamberger's of New Jersey, Abraham & Straus, Rich's of Atlanta, Brooks, Fredrick's of Hollywood, Foley's in Texas, Bikini Village, New England's Jordan Marsh. They no longer supply Bloomingdale's, who, the twins felt, demanded too many changes in suit design. "If you don't desperately need that account, it's best not to do it," states Jackie, speaking of Bloomie's. Saks Fifth Avenue handled their suits for four years, then wanted their own Saks label in them. According to Baird, "They're very square," and consistently managed to choose the least popular styles. Lord & Taylor, on the other hand, are quite the opposite. Baird was impressed with their merchandising and new chic "incredible" store in Chicago.

A blue-chip account, Casual Corner—based in Connecticut, with about three hundred stores in the Northeast—indicates The Twins bathing suits are popular with teen-agers. When asked if they best fit younger women with better figures, one buyer stated, "They best fit women with *no* figures!" The suits are of a style called contemporary, appealing to youthfully shaped females in their early twenties. A size "large" in The Twins line is equivalent to a size ten produced by other manufacturers. This would fit a five-foot-three- to five-foot-six-inch woman weighing approximately 120 to 130 pounds. Large?

At present The Twins, Inc., exports to South America, Central America, the Caribbean islands, and New Guinea. They have no plans to go public; both like being totally in charge. "I would hate to be in a situation where we would have to have board meetings to get anything done," states Gillian.

The golden-tanned women in neat, young-looking sportswear would be an unaccustomed sight in a board room. In fact, they are unusual within the women's-wear manufacturing field. Asked how two WASPs managed to enter the predominantly Jewish "rags" business successfully, Gillian mentions show business, where most agents are Jews: "I wouldn't work for a non-Jewish agent. I wouldn't trust him." They grew up in a Jewish neighborhood in Hove and worked in the Catskills in predominantly Jewish-run resorts. They've enjoyed excellent relationships with Jews, and prospered.

These two women work well together and have carved out a moneymaking enterprise. One reason for this success is their warm personal relationship with each other, their mutual trust. "To have a sister cheat you out of a dime would be too awful," insists Gillian Davis Mitchell.

From the time they were little girls living with their mother, they trusted each other and were close. According to Gillian's Earl Mitchell, they received little love from their mother: "It was probably the most loveless relationship between mother and daughter I've ever heard of. Their mother let them wander through the streets during air raids, didn't worry about them. . . . That is . . . not . . . motherhood. Gill probably misses her mother more than she would like to say, because she still talks about her all the time." A measure of the effect Madeline Davis had upon

Gillian is Earl Mitchell's feelings toward the dead woman he never met: "I resent it when I listen to it [Mrs. Davis's treatment of her children]; I'm almost glad I didn't know her, because I probably wouldn't have liked her."

Jacqueline Baird and Gillian Mitchell married American men, started a business in Florida, and consider it home. Jacqueline says, "I don't think a day goes by when I don't think, I am lucky to live here . . . in the sun and the wind . . . I drive across the Causeway going home and I see the water on each side. I wish more Americans would realize what they've got. I'm not saying this because I've made money here; I loved it when I was broke. . . . Gill and I used to split hot dogs and hamburgers; you know, we had very little money."

Their two homes are both about twenty minutes' ride from the plant in their identical Mercedes-Benzes. The Mitchells live on tiny, hidden Belle Meade Island, between Miami and Miami Beach, and Gillian lives perhaps ten minutes away on another, Normandy Isle, which also sits between the mainland and the shoreline. Neither dwelling is pretentious; the Bairds live with three children and a housekeeper in the more hectic, less organized setting of the two.

When she arrives home, Jacqueline has a cup of tea, English style—with milk and sugar—and spends time with the children; after work, and a tall glass of water, Gillian leaves for the tennis court.

Butch Baird, professional athlete, says the sisters are equal in tennis ability and ranks them among the top six female players in the Miami area. Usually they play with men, for it is hard finding women players of their caliber.

Gillian Mitchell, who is fond of outdoor activities, is an amateur naturalist and visits Alaska, goes on safaris, and has become knowledgeable about spots like the Galápagos Islands with professor-guided tours. "I fell in love with the Galápagos!" she says.

Always ready to display enthusiasm, Mitchell is living energy. "I'm a bit more high-strung than Jackie, an ounce or so, an ounce or so." She struts with a jaunty, almost military gait. The fastest walkers would have trouble keeping up with her. Outspoken, she tends to disagree vehemently when she feels strongly.

Earl Mitchell on his wife: "She doesn't get mad too easy. She can get mad but it takes quite a bit of doing. . . . Very English . . . She never loses control." Jacqueline is similar, says Butch Baird: "Her temper? Very little, very little." Their spouses—who admit, "We compare notes all the time"—find the women easy to live with. Mitchell, when asked why he married Gillian rather than Jacqueline, smiled. "I met her first." By the time he met Jackie, he was already "entranced; I thought there was nobody in the world like Gill, and I haven't found anything to change my mind yet."

The twins compare their spouses as well; they say there is much in common. Referring to her mate, Gillian Mitchell states, "Father sits with his feet up" while she cleans the house, does the dishes, and gets dinner ready. "I resented that very much in the beginning [of my marriage]," says Gillian. Jacqueline Baird agrees. "I found when Butch was home . . . I'd think, Rats, look at him, he's only been practicing golf and he's sitting over there with his bloody feet up and I'm doing the bloody dinner and I worked all day, too!" Gill on the plight of women: "I really admire what Gloria Steinem is doing, but there is no way in the world I could relate to her." Jacqueline Baird agrees: "There's nothing unliberated about *our* lives."

Aside from their husbands and the Baird children, the only family they're in touch with is their deceased father's second wife, Lillie Davis, who lives in Cannes. They feel close to her—she has no children—and travel to France to visit. She comes to their homes for six weeks every year. Unlike Madeline Davis, this mother is easy to love.

Their stepmother, husbands, the three children, and each other. Warm, close relationships. But surely these sisters could not get along all the time. What do you argue about? "Picky, stupid, idiotic little things that are never worth arguing about. . . . You look back and think, What the devil were we talking about?" says Jacqueline Baird. Gillian and Jacqueline seem to agree that their disagreements are insignificant. "I mean we're normal sisters, no?" states Jacqueline in her British boarding-school English.

Both are tolerant and good-natured with each other; they are equally relaxed when people invariably question and compare them. Jackie admits she does it herself when she walks into a room containing twins, and says people feel proud when they guess the correct twin. The mistaken-identification problem is not present when they are apart, although she tells about the first time she met Gillian's husband-to-be: "I opened the door and he had not yet met me, and he said, 'Oh, hi, there, Gill!' Wrong! He laughed and I laughed."

In addition to appearance and interests, their basic strengths and drive are similar. So much in common . . .

Says Butch Baird, in his Western drawl: "Even their gynecologist says they're just alike. He was *amazed*."

3

CERES AND CHARDONNAY

Catherine Clark

———————•◦∞◦•———————

A SVELTE, pleasant-looking woman smiles indiscriminately at consumers from a photograph on Brownberry Ovens' seasoned croutons boxes stacked on the supermarket shelf. Accompanying the gentle face is a synopsis of the Catherine Clark success story:

> Like many of you, I could never accept what commercial bakeries did to those wonderful things our grandmothers used to bake. So, back in 1946 when I was a young wife and new mother in the little town of Oconomowoc, Wisconsin, I decided to do something about it.
>
> I baked my own loaf of freshly ground wheat bread. My neighbors loved it so I offered it for sale in the local shops.
>
> Soon the news spread to the neighboring towns. Then to the big cities.
>
> Vacationers who came to our lovely Wisconsin lake and farm country carried loaves back home with them. Then wrote for more—from all over the country.
>
> Very soon our little bakery (which I named Brownberry Ovens) had outgrown its walls. As time went on, I created more such special

breads. Then dinner and sweet rolls. And finally the special croutons.

Now I hope you don't believe for a moment that one crouton is just as good as another. These are seasoned with my own special recipe. But more importantly, they're made from my genuine Brownberry Ovens bread—and that makes all the difference in the world. . . .

[Signed] Catherine T. Clark

By American standards, Catherine Taft Clark, in her seventies, is considered a senior citizen. To know Mrs. Clark is to laugh at such a label. The dynamic, forceful, intelligent wife and mother, and founder of a multimillion-dollar foods corporation (sold recently to the Peavy Corporation, which retains Clark as chairman of the board) says, "Now that this phase is gone—and I don't really have any authority and it bothers me not to—I'd like to start a new business. . . . I feel sad at having lost the right to make decisions. . . . It drives you crazy. That's the price you pay when you sell." The price Peavy paid when it purchased Brownberry Ovens was twelve million dollars. This thought causes Catherine Clark to smile like a satisfied child.

Down-to-earth and sensible, Catherine was forced by circumstances to think and react like an adult at an early age. She was born in 1907 in Whitewater, Wisconsin, population about 5,000, to Warren and Clara West Taft; their ancestors came west from New York State, then called York State, and traveled to Wisconsin.

Catherine's father, a bit of an entrepreneur, ran a garage and had the only car in town. Before servicing and selling autos, he retailed and repaired bicycles and later had the first movie house in Whitewater. "My mother sold tickets," she recalls, "and I can remember as a small child . . . seeing the first show of everything that ever came out of Hollywood. And then I went out to the car and slept" until her parents finished working for the evening.

It was during the period when he ran the theatre that her father became critically ill. His daughter says: "I'm sure there were heavy debts, for my father was ill and hospitalized. I don't know what he died of, something called Bright's disease [chronic nephritis]. At eight you're impressionable, and I guess my memory is chiefly of seeing him in the coffin." The family, in addition to her mother, consisted of an older brother and a younger brother. Soon after their father died, the Taft residence was sold and a smaller one purchased. Clara Taft—now the sole support of the family—washed neighbors' laundry to feed her family, Catherine reluctantly relates, adding, "Do you think this needs to go into the book? . . . Maybe it's all right. Well, she thought she had to be at home and she had to do things she could do at home and she was not trained for . . . writing a book, for example, and she did people's washings. I don't know what else she could have done. It got me through high school, although I had summer jobs."

Catherine, who does not remember ever being spanked by her parent, says, "I dominated her because I was strong. . . . I'm sure I'm tougher than she was. But she was very kind and very comforting and the kind of mother I suppose old-fashioned people thought mothers should be. She didn't worry about what she was doing."

But her young daughter was ashamed: "After my mother was widowed, the townspeople—I think it was Thanksgiving—came with a basket of food. I wasn't very old and it was probably very kind of them to do that. But after the person left who brought it, I put my head down on the table and cried bitterly. It was absolutely crushing. I don't know why I should have been so proud." Catherine feels do-gooders might find a less demeaning way to help, yet admits her mother appreciated the groceries. "She was just sorry that I reacted."

There were other hurts. The young Catherine felt pain when

excluded from a friend's birthday celebrations because she lived "on the wrong side of the tracks. . . . But," she says, "I don't recall any deprivations, was never hungry. I did wear hand-me-downs . . . from strangers." She had difficulty accepting this.

When Catherine was twelve, her widowed mother thought of remarrying. The child stopped it. "She considered it and I killed it." The man was Catherine's father's brother. "I just made a fuss . . . totally unreasonable. It was the nicest thing that could have happened to her . . . She *was* willing to be talked out of it. I'll have to say that."

From the age of eight until graduation from the Whitewater secondary school, Catherine remembers a happy home and childhood. She says she was headstrong and apt to take risks as a young person: "I never hesitated a minute when invited to ride in an army-surplus World War I biplane. The next week it crashed in Iowa. . . . And I once roller-skated ten miles hanging on to a car. Oh, yes, I can still see those skate wheels worn completely through, and HOT."

She and her mother, a farmer's daughter, were close. "Mom was a very reasonable person, maybe a little easy." When asked if she physically resembles Clara Taft, Catherine, a lithe woman, says, "I don't think so. She had brown eyes, though, and I've got those." Prone to be heavy, Mrs. Taft was not particularly Spartan about how much she ate, and enjoyed cooking and baking for her family. While she was an average five feet four, her husband and his family were extremely tall individuals.

Their daughter Catherine, taking after her paternal side, is a statuesque woman. Five feet eight inches tall when she was in high school, Catherine liked basketball, was team captain, and recalls playing baseball and tennis "wearing bright white bloomers. . . . I was not a cheerleader. I was a participant." The athlete's first high-school crush was Ed Woodward. "His father had a car

and he used nice after-shave lotion." In addition to her interests
in sports and romance, she played the piano "in a funny little
bongo band we had, the Bimbos," and worked her way "from the
end of one shelf to the other" at the library. "I was a reader."

Catherine graduated as valedictorian—"I learned easily. I
wasn't a drudge." She reflects: "I didn't know or wasn't encouraged to think that a girl could work her way through college, and
I felt I had to get a job instead and really help. Which I did." She
had taken a secretarial-clerical course in school, which, she says,
"I could market."

So, as her older brother played saxophone with a dance band to
help pay expenses while he attended the University of Wisconsin
(where he received a football scholarship), Catherine aided with
the support of the home. She marketed her skills as secretary in
the office of a local college president.

It was while she was employed by the school that her fifteen-
year-old brother, Clarence, died of pneumonia. Seven years before, when her father had died, Catherine perhaps did not know
the realities of life. She states today, "I learned fast."

While working at the college she continued her interest in
basketball and, she says, "there was one very good player and I
liked his looks and I guess we were in love." (This woman in her
seventies is delightfully girlish when remembering long-ago ro-
mances. Thoughtful for a moment, she adds, "What's going to
happen when my husband reads this?") The relationship ended
when she moved to Milwaukee and he also relocated. By the time
he phoned her, she had met her husband-to-be. "But I really
loved him. . . . I have no idea what happened to him, but don't
think I haven't wondered. His name was George Heil but he was
called Larry. He was an intellectual, a literary type, as well as a
basketball player. If you ask me, I'll show you his picture in the
yearbook sometime. There are things that he said that I still

remember. . . . I suppose he became a coach. . . . But I'm curious."

Mrs. Taft continued as a laundress until her daughter moved
to Milwaukee to begin working in the personnel department of a
department store. Catherine says of her mother, "I was old
enough to have her come and live with me."

An individual who knew Clara says she was not a bright woman; yet her clever daughter—twenty-six as she took full responsibility for her mother—began working in a department wholly
manned by college graduates, and her intelligence, tenacity, and
drive began to emerge.

During the Depression, her department was, according to
Catherine, "cut down to the bone." Hired as an experiment to
evaluate the untrained high-schooler—Catherine—versus the
college graduate, she was one of a handful not fired when business took a downward turn, while university-trained employees
were let go.

Owing to the cutbacks, she now had to work in all three of the
company's stores. "I had a little Model A and traveled between
locations in Milwaukee." Her responsibilities included writing
trade manuals for each department, training salespeople, and
editing a house organ. She also arranged fashion shows. A light
quick laugh erupts as she remembers the variety of chores. "It was
mighty interesting. I loved what I was doing," she says, in her
quiet, refined way.

While living in Milwaukee with her mother, she met Russell
Clark on a blind date: "There was a girl . . . who was much
wealthier . . . who had parties and invited me to a New Year's
party and invited Russell, my [future] husband."

Russell Clark, a graduate of a Wisconsin liberal arts school,
was working before attending Harvard to earn a master's in business administration. They corresponded while he was in Cam-

bridge. When he returned two years later he worked in Chicago for the Northern Trust Company. Then at the bottom of the Depression he changed jobs, "which seemed to be folly." Catherine thinks perhaps he did so because she was in Milwaukee and he wished to be with her. "I'm not really sure, but he *did* get a job in Milwaukee."

They were married, and the newlyweds settled in the lakefront town of Oconomowoc, a watering place for Detroiters and Milwaukeeans (it is one hour west of Milwaukee) during the nineteenth century. The Clarks bought a home and moved in, Mrs. Taft included.

After her marriage, Catherine continued in the personnel department until she and Russell decided to begin a family. In 1935, red-headed Sue Cassidy Clark was born followed by Penelope three years later. Grandmother Clark, a loving and stable individual, was in the home and available to watch over the children as the thirty-four-year-old Catherine began to get itchy feet.

Russell Clark recalls the early 1940s when his wife "wanted to establish a children's shop or something," and Catherine counters, "I didn't dwell very long on *that*." Russell: "No." Catherine remembers: "The whole town knew I was going to do something but nobody knew what it was. And when they heard it was going to be a bakery—well, nothing very prestigious about *that*. That's what *they* thought. . . . They were wrong." Her voice rises slightly at the end of this statement, accentuating her "I showed *them*" attitude.

A local village bakery sold bread Catherine found unusually good. The name of the breadmaker was on the package. She approached the man—Mr. Marsh—and stated she wished to purchase his wheat-bread recipe. He agreed to sell it. So she promptly rented a store, purchased an old beer delivery truck, and began what eventually became Brownberry Ovens. Equipment was obtained from Mr. Marsh; her first mixer made twelve loaves at a time. "In three months I had outgrown the equipment."

Regarding the initial capital, Catherine says, "Russ was making a medium income. It wasn't great but . . . it was above average. . . ." A low-key cynic, she mentions she was finally living on the *right* side of the tracks. However, funds were not easily available to lease a store, purchase a bread recipe, and buy a truck and equipment. So Catherine convinced her husband they should borrow the money by mortgaging their home. "I guess he thought I was smart." In addition, a couple of friends who, she says, felt "Russell's honest and Catherine's bright" put some cash toward the venture. Russell, she says, is a conservative, and she adds, "I'm the risk-taker."

This woman bought a certain loaf of wheat bread in a grocery store, approached the baker, and set up a business about which she had absolutely no knowledge, experience, or information. "I'm an opportunist," she admits. "Part of doing a good job in business is to recognize a chance when you see it." The year was 1946, right after V-J Day. Women at that time stayed home, pleased that their husbands earned a livable salary, and bore and cared for children. Catherine Taft Clark saw things differently: "I don't remember any particular excitement . . . it seemed like a normal course of events. . . . I guess it's the idea that if you think you can do something, it's a crime not to do it, it's a shame not to do it. . . . I don't think I defined it that clearly at the time. But I thought I could do it and I thought—"

Question: You thought it might be fun?

Answer: "Fun? I thought it might make some money."

Capitalization was low. She explains in her clipped, precise manner of speech, pronouncing every "t," "It was partly necessity

and partly fortuitous that we bought used equipment," for during the war years no civilian manufacturing apparatus was built.
She designed a "Brownberry Ovens" label and hired the woman
who previously helped in the house, along with the Clarks'
former handyman: "He was a good worker and a good mechanic,
though not a very easy person to get along with," but the machinery was large, requiring muscle to operate and maintain, and
a male was a necessary addition to the beginning enterprise. And
every other day this employee drove to Milwaukee to make de-
liveries in the secondhand beer truck. Doris—the ex-
housemaid—was, according to Catherine, "such a nice person
and a good worker," and the two of them toiled together. Says
Catherine: "I call myself a grubber. You grub along for a while
before you start doing things 'just like downtown.' [The first in-
vestment] was fairly precious. When you realize that you've
mortgaged your house—Russ was very willing that we should do
that—you watch your expenditures carefully. We had secondhand things. I don't know that I had anything new. . . . We
actually started in little batches. . . . We wrapped the bread by
hand in waxed paper and had a string-tier to close the end of the
package." She tucked her label under the wax-paper wrapper. "I
don't know how Mrs. Rudkin did hers at Pepperidge, but that's
what I did."

Russell Clark kept a simple ledger in his spare time and
Catherine remembers, "We had some big accounts in Milwaukee
who wanted to be billed; the rest were cash. It was very elementary." At one point, Russ drove to northern Michigan, looked
over equipment for sale, went home and reported its condition to
Catherine and her male helper. The ex-handyman said he could
make the equipment usable. So six months after starting the
business Brownberry Ovens purchased machinery enabling them
to produce larger quantities. One day after the new purchase

arrived, Catherine was sitting on the floor disassembling a large piece of the machinery that required a thorough cleaning. A customer walked in the door. She still remembers the astonishment on his face as he found her in dirty overalls doing this job. "They talked about it for years," states Catherine, with glee, of the Oconomowoc townspeople.

Her Oconomowoc neighbors reacted variously to this businesswoman in their midst. "I could tell those who had truly friendly feelings, because when I'd meet them on the street they were very much interested and excited and asked me how I was doing. The others never mentioned it. They ignored it."

But Wisconsin residents and other Midwesterners did not snub her product. A reason for Catherine's ultimate success with Brownberry Ovens was her distinctive baked goods free of preservatives or artificial ingredients well before the time consumers considered such problems. And Brownberry Ovens bread was, and is, delicious. "I thought I could do it, that there was a need. The basis of all businesses is to find a real need," she says. "I thought it was pretty chancy and that there was enough risk not to count on making money," and she remembers thinking, If it goes, it could be a profitable enterprise.

While Catherine worked at the bakery, her mother was home with the now school-age girls. "I really have to say my going into business was eased considerably by having a grandmother" in the house. Catherine also tried to arrange her work schedule to be through with her day's efforts when Sue and Penelope arrived home. Often they came to the shop after school. "I don't know whether the girls felt deprived; maybe they did," she says. "I felt guilty because of what mothers of their contemporaries thought." With a smile she adds, "I bought Twinkies. I didn't make a cake. I haven't much defense." Both daughters say there was no particular problem having two working parents. According to

Catherine, "There was dust above the doors and other house-keeping lapses." Did her husband mind? Russell states: "Not much." Catherine adds, "When he cared, he did it [the house-work]."

Catherine Clark recollects, "For years I was up to my elbows in dough," yet making and remaking the same recipe never bored her. She considers breadmaking a talent. "When you work with a living organism, the damnedest things happen to it. The weather changes, the barometer changes."

Dough-related problems occurred constantly, yet Brownberry Ovens prospered. Catherine carefully acknowledges her husband's support of her business attempt. One evening someone did not show up for work, so when Russell came home from his day's work at the bank he went to the bakery and "pitched in all night. I don't know how he was at work the next day. . . ." When the time came to market their product to new outlets, the two of them would, according to Russell, "go out and sell bread on Saturdays." Catherine says, "Oh, yes, let me tell you about that. We'd take a bunch of samples in the car and drive up to places like Eau Claire, La Crosse, Chicago. Russ would usually take in a breadboard—the bread was not sliced—and a jar of butter." Russ continues unemotionally: "You didn't even have to slice it. All you had to do was put the bread in front of a man and let him look at the bread and it sold itself."

Although her natural products were marketed only in the Midwest—without preservatives they could not be shipped distances—Brownberry Ovens showed a sizable profit after several years. Clark remembers when her bread first came out, Wonder Bread was selling for nineteen cents and she decided to market hers for twenty-two. "One of the things that has never frightened me was to charge whatever it cost. I didn't take a salary in the very beginning." At one point, an excess-profit law was passed by Congress: a business could net twenty-five thousand dollars more than it did the year before; any money above that amount would be heavily taxed. Catherine Clark's business had made practically no money in previous years, so this first period of sizable profits required heavy business-related spending to avoid the tax. Clark decided it was time to advertise.

A camera bug, Catherine photographed settings including a basket of bread, her grandmother's clock, and her old red checked tablecloth. She presented these to a Milwaukee agency, and her first advertising campaign began. "That's just how the ads came out. They were placed in the rotogravure section of the Milwaukee *Journal*. It was the brown section; this ad was in color, 'just like downtown.'" (Another often-used old-fashioned phrase: "Maybe you'll call uncle.") With exposure and a delicious product, Brownberry Ovens was on its way.

Catherine remained instrumental in the advertising. "I was the boss. I was the king. I could do everything I wanted. I thought I had a flair for advertising and I worked with the agency personally. The sales manager—when I got one—was with me, but I still had the last word." She saw her trailer trucks as "moving billboards. The first time I saw one with my name in such big letters, it was somewhat overwhelming."

Catherine Clark feels the basic key to success is an outstanding product, but she also believes in capitalizing on the touches which help an item sell. For years she participated as a corporation in an annual food editors' conference. Each manufacturer at these gatherings does its best to attract the public's attention, "And so did we. But I think we were a little more creative. . . . We've been *very* successful." Once, Brownberry Ovens staged a Sunday morning breakfast (on a Thursday) at a Neiman-Marcus store and served breakfasts with recipes from all over the country. Another year, Brownberry served at the Goodman Theatre, con-

nected with the Chicago Art Museum: "It was quite original."
According to Clark, her skit in the theatre, based upon a lost
generation of women who do not know how to bake, was
aimed toward the mothers of today's college kids. Then breakfast
was eaten in the kitchen.

At one point, Brownberry Ovens—under Catherine's
direction—launched a campaign to teach people to bake bread at
home. This doesn't make sense if you want them to buy your
bread, though, does it? "You'd think so, but it does. It's very
subtle." In connection with this, she wrote *Bread Baking: The
How and Why Book*, distributed by Brownberry. As tightly written, yet with a personalized, homey feeling, is her salad booklet.
And her recipes work. She launched a series of advertising and
public relations campaigns to do with what she calls endangered
food species: old-fashioned lemon meringue pie made with lots of
eggs; buckwheat cakes served with sorghum; buttermilk that isn't
cultured; snow ice cream; sausage made whole with all good
seasonings; cream cheese without gum; gooseberry pie.

"I still think it was one of my brighter moments," states Clark
when complimented on the double entendre of the name of a
new product, Health Nut Bread, and says she invented her bran
bread because others on the market taste like sawdust; her recipe
gets past that problem by adding whole ground-up oranges.

As Brownberry Ovens sales volume grew, Catherine Clark received publicity from the national news media. Articles have
appeared concerning her since 1954. One was titled "The
Woman Behind the Bread; Catherine Clark Succeeds in a Man's
World." A 1960 *Wall Street Journal* ran a series on new millionaires and included "Road to Riches: Costly Loaf of Bread
Helps Catherine Clark Build Bakery Fortune." A news clip de-
scribing Mrs. Clark stated, "She is fast becoming a producer of a
national market; franchising and mail orders are her means of

reaching the hungry millions.... Write for a sample—she'll mail you the sweetest bread you ever tasted!" A clever public-relations item was a *Harvard Business School Bulletin* piece, published in the summer of 1954, titled "The Brownberry Bread of Catherine Clark," by Russell J. Clark, '27, who allows that Catherine had more to do with the writing than he did. He says she inserts a bit of levity into his writing. Gives it some zip. He feels she is a very clever, capable writer. With her usual straightforwardness, she simply declares, "I wrote it." An exerpt from that 1954 article:

> A few years ago, if anyone had referred to a "proof box" in my hearing, I would have assumed he referred to photography; an allusion to "primary fermentation" would have suggested to my mind the industries for which Milwaukee is famous. All that is changed now. My wife (who sometimes refers to herself as a "maladjusted housewife"), responding to the new freedom brought about by the mechanization of almost every household task, as well as her own disinclination to become too involved in the few that remained, went into business. Started as a sideline—a hobby if you will—this business is in danger of grossing a million dollars next year....
>
> I would like to tell you a little about my wife—not too much because she'll read this and become too big for her boots if I go overboard.... She was ... ready to settle down, raise a family, and do the family baking. At least, that's what I thought. She went through a Club Period: Women's, Garden, Bridge, Reading, Sewing, and a stint as Girl Scout Commissioner. I should add, in passing, that she is a good dancer, plays jazz by ear—Debussy by note—and paints charmingly in water colors.... The children adore her and are very proud of what she has accomplished. Needless to say, this is true of her husband as well.

The Harvard article goes on to describe Catherine's views on breadmaking:

Catherine subscribes to the theory that the pulverizing or macerating of the germ which results from fine-grinding of whole wheat flours dissipates its value through loss of the volatile oils. She is also a purist with regard to honest wheat flavor which she feels should *never* be covered up by the stronger flavors of molasses, honey, invert sugar syrup, etc.

The original loaf was hailed with great enthusiasm. . . .

During the ensuing years, used equipment was gradually replaced by new, the old store building . . . was . . . added to; a neighboring building was leased; warehouses were rented; the thirdhand repainted beer truck has been replaced by a fleet of nineteen fine trucks . . . [and a] . . . building was erected on a three-acre tract. . . .

For the first 4 years the company either doubled, or more than doubled, its previous year's sales . . . our total work-force has grown from two employees . . . to 72. This represents a not inconsiderable payroll, most of which is spent in Oconomowoc. And what is even nicer, most of these people are our friends and neighbors from surrounding homes and farms. . . .

For the first 5 years we spent no money—had none to spend!—on printed advertising, radio or TV. We did package sample slices of bread which were distributed . . . in a wonderful door-to-door campaign worked out by Catherine and her club member friends. These ladies, obviously not ordinary doorbell-punchers, almost invariably were encouraged to give their sales pitch, and like as not were invited in. They still regale their friends with some of their more harrowing adventures! Waukesha, Oconomowoc, and the better sections of Madison and Milwaukee were blanketed in this way. We are convinced that where taste and flavor are truly outstanding, this method of getting the consumer to take her first bite is highly effective. . . . [At stores, fairs, etc.] we use a . . . demonstrator dressed in the costume of our trademark girl, who makes fresh buttered toast and offers it to passersby. . . .

A tongue-in-cheek element was interjected by an illustration which originally appeared in a Harvard Business School bulletin.

On Having a Wife in Business

CON'S

1. Busy wife produces no cakes, pies or other Culinary Triumphs.

2. Social life reduced to a minimum.

3. No spare time for golf, leaf raking, trap shooting.

4. Vacations become business trips.

5. Deprived of wife's company while she attends conventions or makes business trips.

6. Strong tendency to bore friends with shop talk.

7. Dust settles and remains between weekly visits of cleaning-lady.

8. Tired wife not always good company.

9. Have to listen to bad puns on "banker" and "baker" and "dough"; and sly remarks about lucky fellows who put their wives out to work.

PRO'S

1. Weight control made easier.

2. True friends have survived neglect. Situation improving as we grow large enough to hire competent management assistants. Many new and interesting people added to our circle.

3. Couldn't want more fascinating hobby. Recreational, for me.

4. More widely travelled than normally would be, with business to help pay the freight.

5. Wife so busy has no time to develop symptoms, ailments, psychoses.

6. Helpful suggestions and ideas come from well wishers who invariably *open* the subject.

7. Wife has some trouble finding time to buy clothes, spend money.

8. I get tired, too. Glad she doesn't always want to go out.

9. Conversation at home quite stimulating, as a rule. Considerable satisfaction in seeing a small initial investment grow. An augmented family income isn't hard to take, either.

(Courtesy of the *Harvard Business School Bulletin*

As the illustrated page suggests, Catherine Clark sees financially-achieving wives as a trial to their husbands—no matter how liberated the male—for society has not yet decided how to react to the self-made wife, and to her spouse, who occasionally acts jealous, tends to take credit or answer questions directed toward the wife, and wonders, Is she a better man than I? Though it can be a cause of stressful episodes within a marriage, Catherine says the males tend to deny it strenuously. "The emasculation of husbands," she calls it, and says, "I don't know what to do about it. I have no answers. Because I feel strongly that women are individuals. They're people and have just as much right to egos and success as anyone. And any man who thinks of them as chattel or property is wrong."

Catherine Taft Clark, founder of the Brownberry Ovens, has often been quoted as saying that a man given her taste buds and possessing her intangible talent could have built his organization sooner than she did hers. Previously she stated a male would have obtained her success in one-half the time it took her. "Well, I'm going to modify that to one-third," she says today. She recognizes problems connected with her femininity. "I've been trying to build my management team for many years and I took what I could get. I'd pick a good man and he'd decide he did not want to work for a woman. There was a problem. Oh, yes. Slows you down." (Another day, Catherine comments, "Funny how men are always waited on," as she and a woman friend serve their menfolk her delicious strawberry shortcake.)

When she formed her company in the forties, it was not considered ladylike to be financially successful. Professional accomplishment was more in keeping with a woman's place. Yet Clark is pleased she made money. And proud. Straight-backed, with erect yet graceful posture and gray hair, the proper, wealthy-looking woman exudes confidence. Warm and affectionate, she is at the same time covertly, smoothly manipulative, but in an intelligent manner, which, if one is even aware of it, commands respect. Her delightful dry sense of humor and aristocratic manner of speech give the impression that she is more attractive than she actually is, physically speaking.

With the high-spirited pace of a graceful racehorse, Catherine Taft Clark appears years younger than her age, and she loves it when someone says so. She dresses beautifully and simply, and says, "I weigh a hundred and twenty-six, except sometimes I weigh a hundred and thirty if I'm not paying attention. If I'm tasting a lot of rich pastry and I'm really working on something—I adore butter and buttery things—I tend to not watch my weight much." Her husband, a master of understatement and often reluctant to hand out compliments, says that when he met her "she was quite handsome. I don't know if I'd call her a beauty." Of her mind he comments, "She's grown. The capacity was there. Always."

In 1972, at the time of its sale to Peavy for twelve million dollars, Brownberry Ovens was distributing about twelve breads, a half-dozen rolls, and a variety of stuffings and croutons to the north-central Middle West, chiefly the areas of the Twin Cities, Wisconsin, and Chicago. In the last year of Clark's reign prior to connecting with Peavy, Brownberry netted a quarter of a million dollars. (Profits have declined slightly since Catherine stepped down.) She continued to be "Brownberry Oven's Catherine Clark," the public-relations image of the firm, lecturing and appearing on radio and television shows.

Corporate decisions were a part of her life for over thirty years. She now has more time for her family—Russell, her husband, and adult daughters, Sue and Penny.

Sue Cassidy Clark, a sports and rock-music photojournalist, lives in New York City, and Penny sells antiques in San Francisco, specializing in stained glass. Their parents provided trusts for the women, and Catherine muses on whether this was a supportive move or a negative action in terms of her children's growth and happiness.

When asked if being the child of a super-successful mother adversely affected them, the women—both in their early forties—did not have ready answers. Russell considered for a full twenty seconds. "Probably not." He then thought about the possibility of their being affected positively by a mother who is the model of an achieving woman. After a full fifteen-second pause, he mused inconclusively, "How can you tell?"

Intimidated or impressed—or both—her children see Catherine as unusual, a domineering, forceful individual. "Yes, she is. She is a *very* strong person," says Sue, who takes after Clark in this respect, which led to conflicts as Sue was growing up and which, she says, "I understand better now. But she's *too* successful in *everything*." Her mother draws, creates, sews, and conducts business. She's a wonderwoman. "Oh, yes, she really is," Sue says, and adds that her mother wants to live forever. "I admire that."

Penelope Clark—who, like Sue, speaks in what Saul Bellow refers to as "fashionable Eastern lockjaw manner"—compares her mother to a mongoose. Tenacious animals, they grab onto something, according to Penny, and keep shaking it, and just won't let go. If Catherine Clark is in fact a mongoose type, she is a very composed, confident, and soft-spoken one.

Neither daughter is married. "I used to bug them but I stopped," states Catherine, and, "Thank God," counter her offspring. Catherine Clark would "recommend children, if asked," for her single daughters. "Having children is perhaps the greatest experience in my whole life," she says. She admits, however, that possibly she wants grandchildren to satisfy her own ego. Sue

Catherine Clark in publicity photo prior to sale of Brownberry Ovens, Inc. to the Peavy Corporation

changes the subject and starts discussing the merits of cats. "Shh," commands Mother with mock seriousness.

The Clarks maintain a slower life-style now than they used to. Russell always helped with the house chores as his wife was establishing her corporation, and he still pitches in. Catherine, an excellent cook, fusses over her meals, carefully warming dishes to the proper temperature. All is done with precision and to the point of perfection in their home, which is now in San Francisco; the couple moved there when Russell retired. In addition to a town house on Russian Hill, Catherine and her husband own an infant vineyard—Icaria Vineyard—filled with Chardonnay vines in Sonoma County. When she is not flying back and forth, once a month, to Oconomowoc, Wisconsin—"I get more work done on the plane than anyplace"—for two weeks' work at the Brownberry headquarters, she spends the weekdays in San Francisco, and the couple travels about sixty miles north of San Francisco for weekends.

In Sonoma, their casual home—they call it "the ranch"—is surrounded by beautifully landscaped areas and an extensive vegetable garden. Her living room overlooks a heated pool near gazebos with ornamental iron furnishings. A backdrop is formed for the vineyard beyond the swimming area by a series of hills poking above the redwoods. The guest house has a trellis with Thompson grapes where hummingbirds hover motionless before red liquid-filled feeders. In addition to the grapes, Catherine grows almonds, tomatoes, Swiss chard, peaches, hops—she plans to experiment with them in bread—and herbs. In addition to the guest house, there is a sauna outbuilding on the 350-acre plot. The lawn is manicured.

The place is secluded, spotlessly neat, and organized. The Clarks intend for Icaria Vineyard to become a wine-producing property. Catherine has the label design in mind: "And on the back it'll have the whole story." Her croutons, remember, have her tale of accomplishment on the box. She named the vineyard for French utopians who settled near their stream in the 1800s.

In San Francisco with Russell, weekends among the Chardonnay grapevines, and the remainder of the month in Oconomowoc. Her Wisconsin home—Brownberry House, a charming early-nineteenth-century structure with a porch swing and flower beds—has the Brownberry Ovens bakery in its back yard. A glance out the comfortably decorated rear guest room unexpectedly encounters a Brownberry Mack truck. Nearby, the factory entrance is graced by a garden area—raspberries, vegetables, cherry trees, flowers—planted by Catherine. Inside the bakery hangs a picture of Brownberry's founder. On a table, a memo pad still carries her printed thought: "Avoid oral instructions." The delightfully fragrant large back work area is filled with active employees in paper bakers' caps or white hairnets.

Several blocks from the bakery, bench-sitting teen-agers and a strolling elderly couple enjoy a park which before Catherine's intervention was an unused lot. Garbage and rubbish had been accumulating and the land was being wasted; Catherine cannot stand squander. Through her efforts, the citizenry created the vest-pocket park.

Catherine enjoys beautiful surroundings, indoors and out. While she is not an extravagant spender on clothing, her husband says she likes to be in style. Catherine adds, "I like good jewelry. I'll spend a lot of money on a strand of pearls," and she considers: "I never do anything ordinary. My husband one day suggested I buy a Cadillac. I said, 'Oh, God, I wouldn't be seen *dead* in a Cadillac.' He didn't quite get what I meant. I feel always that I'm unique and that the things I do in life are mine. . . . Whatever kind of ego this is, I don't know. But there it is."

Catherine Clark is an unusual woman. This high-school

graduate who serves on the board of governors at St. Mary's College, "as close as I got to some education," ponders, "Is there any answer to the fact that I still have lots of steam and it's not being utilized? I'd like to be on a board of directors somewhere." In the eighth decade of life, she states, "I don't know what I'm going to do next," and mentions politics. When speaking and dreaming of starting a new company, she explains she would need a "young strong guy, who's got some experience but no creativity, who would do my bidding." It sounds as though she's lining up a consort. She considers her built-in handicaps— "namely, age"—when mulling things over concerning her future, and mentions that perhaps she could go to college. "I might do that, as a matter of fact."

Mrs. Clark is not averse to new experiences. A recent trip to an Arizona tennis camp did not include Russell, who, in his words, feels, "At my age I shouldn't try to play tennis." Catherine describes her tennis experience: ". . . loved it. I took an hour's lesson at eight in the morning and another in the afternoon, but I did not go through the clinic, which is terribly strenuous, about six hours a day. . . . I just figured caution was indicated. I'm not sure I won't go back and go to the clinic later on."

In addition to athletic interests, she enjoys antiquing and is building a collection of pictures of Ceres, ancient goddess of agriculture, who throughout the centuries was connected with annual festivals celebrated in secret, by women. The prints Catherine owns show Ceres surrounded by wheat shafts and a sickle. These could perhaps be the symbols of Catherine's life, who, as she looks back remembering, feels as if another individual lived through her experience: "You *were* someone else. You're not the same person any more. You've changed that much. What you did goes into the pot and makes you what

you've become. . . . I don't believe how old I am, for example."
Old? This woman is as young and bright as a teen-ager. When
told she looks youthful, "Oh, why, thank you. That's the nicest
thing you could say. . . . I'm going to live forever, of course."
Said lightly by the woman whose daughter calls her a superwoman.

The superwoman tag is apparently attached by others as well.
On a sunny June afternoon, as Clark discussed Icaria Vineyard
matters with her foreman (an intelligent greyhound might look at
the man as Catherine does, listening, analyzing), he said to her,
in his Western twang, "I was going to hire a hundred people to
pick the peas, but now that you're here I won't have to."

4

THE KLINGSBORG CONNECTION

Constance Boucher

WHEN SHE was a child, Constance Klingsborg once coerced her sister to trade a tarnished dime for her shiny penny. And Connie's been influencing others to do things her way ever since.

Constance Klingsborg Boucher, with pale blue eyes and long baby blond hair worn in a 1950s severe French twist, radiates softness, roundness, femininity. Oddly, when coiffed in the more girlish dangling ringlets and spit curls for an evening gala, hardness and toughness are accentuated. But whatever façade is visible, the woman exudes competence.

And energy. Boucher—gifts, toys, novelties manufacturer/distributor, rights licensor and licensee—"operates in her own time zone," according to an ex-employee. "It doesn't matter if the sun's up or down." A niece-in-law says, "Connie is on an internal high, a perpetual high. It's incredible. At three in the morning, a new business idea. It almost turns you on to business." It was not always that way, perhaps? Wrong, according to Eve Klingsborg, Constance's mother and employee. Connie was that way in her toddler years.

Her mother was born in Winnipeg, Canada, and her father was from Minnesota; all four grandparents grew up in Sweden. Eve and Frans Klingsborg lived in the Scandinavian area of Ballard, in Seattle, in 1923 when their oldest child, Constance, was born. Mr. Klingsborg was a woodworker and, says his family, designed and built unusually creative furnishings. When asked if her father is still living, Connie says wistfully, "No, he isn't. We miss him. He was really kind of a dynamite person." Mrs. Klingsborg comments: "Connie probably got her artistic talent from him because he worked with his hands . . . and he couldn't draw a curve that wasn't a beautiful curve. He could make anything that was made out of wood; he enjoyed the feel of the wood, the texture, the grain, the smell, the whole thing. But aside from that he was very interested in science . . . archaeology." One observes Connie's mother, widow Eve—softly feminine—and anticipates a Swedish accent. An acquaintance says, "You look at the color of her hair and you wish that you had it . . . pure white . . . you just want to go up and touch it."

Connie remembers her childhood as an "extremely affectionate time." The unhappy part was the poverty, which "made a drastic impression" on both her and her sister June, who is eleven months younger. As the Depression hit, her father lost his Seattle business. "Everything went," states the older daughter, and the family moved from Washington to California searching for work. When they arrived, the Klingsborgs had an old car, fifty dollars, and two kids. "And no work. It was really tough, I remember that," says Connie, and she recalls the family living in back of the Klingsborgs' shop and having no hot water, no rugs . . . nothing the other kids had: ". . . but we had love and affection. I was always conscious of our parents touching each other and being extremely close. A lot of sitting on laps and hugging . . . and it didn't dawn on me until much later that people weren't that physical. And I felt sorry for them."

Their mother remembers: "We dragged those kids everywhere we went. We went to the beach a lot. We camped out." Mrs. Klingsborg—who looks as if she stepped out of the set for *I Remember Mama*—is difficult to envision in a pup tent. It is easy to imagine her loving, hugging, kissing. She continues, "When they were little, we would read to them and sing." And Connie says, "As kids, we got a very good background of literature and reading. We were read *Winnie-the-Pooh, Wind in the Willows* . . . always."

As a child, Connie Klingsborg was on the chubby side. "I was always rounder," says Connie. A vigorous body. She and her tall willowy sister shared a room and, according to June, "I used to keep the tidy half of the room and Connie's was very relaxed." Connie laughs and adds, "To say the least." Connie had half of the closet where she kept her shoes. June: "I'll never forget. She had suède shoes. A gray pair, a green pair, a red pair, and my shoes were very conservative." She says Connie, a shoe-lover, was a "far-out dresser as a kid."

In high school Connie ran for the president of the girls' student body. "I lost, by the way. Too outspoken, I think. Just said the wrong things. I never got that close to the whole group." One of her strongest remembrances is of a San Mateo, California, classroom. Because she was not paying attention, the teacher confronted her: "Connie Klingsborg, you will never amount to anything."

While her mother advanced from being a Girl Scout volunteer to the county director of Girl Scout activities, Connie was busy with her own enterprises, even in grammar school: "I always have been interested in business, you know? From way back. I mean, I used to set everybody's hair on the block. All the ladies would come in. I'd line them all up, wash their hair, wash . . . and set all their hair, and I'd get fifty cents. You know, weird things like this. When I look back, I think, My God, there was always energy that had to be used in some direction. I was always making something, or building something."

During her high-school years, she held summer jobs which often continued into the year. After graduation, she attended a local junior college and sold gloves in a San Mateo department store where she was such a super salesperson that, she says, "I won no friends at all. They had me transferred to another department." She sold more gloves as a weekend worker than the regular women did during the week. People wanting a pair of short white gloves walked out with five or six pairs. "This was in the big glove era, you know?" Eventually she worked in departments throughout the store. And loved it. "I even sold in the basement. Notions. Can you imagine selling notions, needles and pins?" Mrs. Klingsborg remembers, "She was enthusiastic about everything. And it's contagious. She was a natural salesperson."

While Connie was still attending high school and working part time, she met John Boucher. "I think that was my first romance. We were high-school sweethearts," says Connie, with flourishes. As he left for Stanford University, she entered a community college and later went to art school. "The war kind of happened in there somewhere," says Connie, who has difficulty remembering dates and sequences of events.

John Boucher was studying Japanese at Stanford University, where the U. S. Army's Japanese-language school was established; he entered the service and was attached to the school. "Intelligence thing," remembers Connie. "I really never wanted to get

married. . . . *He* wanted to get married and I didn't care whether I
ever got married, really. I kind of had qualms. . . ."

She wed Boucher in Minnesota at Fort Snelling during the
Second World War. She says, "I was twenty, I guess, or twenty-
one."

She says her husband was an "extremely bright guy, very intelligent, with a high I.Q.," who pronounced his name *Bow-
chur*. Someone told her, "You don't pronounce the name cor-
rectly. We're going to call you *Boo-chay*." Years later, sister June,
her husband, and the Bouchers, involved in the Stevenson campaign, attended a reception where June introduced the Bouchers
to Adlai Stevenson: "I'd like you to meet my sister Connie *Boo-
chay* and her husband, John *Bow-chur*." Constance Boucher,
who continues to pronounce it *Boo-chay* today, laughs, and her
plump, vigorous body rocks: "Isn't that a beauty?" When asked
what John Boucher did for a living, she kids, "That's a good
question." He worked for the Christmas Club in his twenties,
"but he pretty much always wanted to retire."

John and Connie's son Douglas was born in Maryland during
the last year of the war as the military intelligence mechanism
was dismantling. The three Bouchers moved back to San Mateo
where Connie continued her warm relationship with her mother.
At one point the Klingsborg women—Constance, June, and
Eve—resided on the same street, next door to one another.
"Those Klingsborg girls and their mother," Connie remembers
people saying. "They've *got* to be too much." As for the sisters'
spouses: "I don't think they loved it. I don't think they liked it at
all," remembers Connie.

A second son, Theodore, was born in San Mateo and, Connie
says, "I got to going to work very quickly because I found I had
time. I had Evie . . . and I could go to work for a few hours every
day."

Prior to her marriage and after art school, she had worked in Los Angeles interior-decorating establishments, and again found employment in an interior-design shop. One of her customers ultimately became the manager of the Joseph Magnin Store in San Mateo; this customer suggested Connie work at the specialty shop as a window dresser. "It sounded like more fun that what I was doing." While designing window displays, she met Magnin's employee James Young, who also became friendly with John Boucher. Referring to herself and Jim Young, she says, "We always liked the same things."

Before her second son's birth, Connie was active in charitable organizations. Later, while she was employed at Joseph Magnin's, her involvement with the Children's Home Society, an adoption agency, catalyzed the eventual formation of her company, Determined Productions. One Halloween, she recalls, "I came up actually with the idea of haunting a house," as a fund-raising event. "I said, 'Let's get an old Victorian, Charles Addams-like house . . . and let's get all the department stores'" to direct their display people to get involved. Connie decreed: "Everyone takes a room and everybody haunts it."

The project became professional and slick. Sound effects. Radio promotion. Newspaper feature articles. "And it was creative. And it was unusual." Her face becomes animated as she remembers. And she coordinated it. "Yes . . ." She pauses, then continues, "And the rest of the gals . . . In about three days, we raised about ten thousand dollars." The successful event was copied throughout the country, and is still held yearly in San Mateo.

After the haunted house, Boucher conceived a second fund-raiser, a Noah's Ark—if she could procure an old barge in Santa Rosa and bring it down to the wharf. Several people told her, "You're not going to be able to tie that old barge up. The

longshoremen won't let you." Yet in the end Connie Boucher
had the Coast Guard helping, and the longshoremen "were fan-
tastic." Others maintained it was against the rules, "It's never
been done," "They'll never give you a berth to dock anything like
this," but Boucher says, "The thing is, most people won't *ask*.
They're afraid to because they're afraid somebody's going to say
no. Usually the answer is yes." Then she reconsiders: "I think you
have to convince people it can be done."

The barge was transformed; an artist designed a Noah's Ark
coloring book to sell on the barge. Boucher approached a printer
to reproduce the books. "We printed by mistake—we didn't know
what we were getting into—a coloring book of the scenes we had
created on the Ark. That was our first venture."

While organizing the haunted house and the Ark, she con-
tinued working in Joseph Magnin's, often with James Young.
Young was involved in the original Halloween scheme, and
Boucher drew him into her newest project as well.

The Noah's Ark coloring book became popular. Boucher decided that, in addition to selling the item at the Ark itself, the
charity's profits would increase if the book was marketed in local
department stores. Joseph Magnin's agreed to stock it and she
approached other businesses: "It wasn't really scary for me. I
walked up to the buyer and explained our Noah's Ark down at the
wharf." Several stores began to offer the item, a regular-sized
coloring book with "fresh new bold artwork," says Boucher.

This could be a business. Let's get into business, she thought as
she recognized the potential of well-drawn coloring books. With
James Young—artistic, creative—and husband, John, Connie
formed a corporation. Determined Productions. Connie says,
"John came up with that name, my ex-husband, because he said,
'That's all you guys have got. Determination.'"

Boucher had determination on all levels. She became upset

with the San Mateo school district, which "was going to start busing the kids . . . almost *to* segregate them. They didn't say that but I knew they were going to do that." Her solution: she took her kids—ages ten and twelve—and went with sister June Dutton and her two youngsters to Switzerland. "I've always had the wanderlust. . . . I had been working at Magnin's and had saved everything I had made over a long period of time. . . . We left our husbands at home." They lived in Switzerland for half the year. It was in Zurich that she recognized a new merchandising concept developing—the gift market. "There were so many exciting things that looked good all over the world and could be sold in the United States." According to Boucher, the gift-item market "was a fluky kind of thing. It was just starting in America but was going to become big business."

Returning to the United States, she approached Magnin's and interested them in the general concept of a true gift-shop department. At the time, she was not sure exactly what her part was going to be in this. Supply the merchandise? Make items? Manufacture? Create new gift ideas? In the late fifties, prior to the huge gift-industry business that developed over the next twenty years, most stores did not have gift-item areas. Connie Boucher thought she could create and make money within such a field. Magnin's was intrigued. "Now," Connie says, "everyone has huge gift departments."

At the same time, her successful Noah's Ark coloring book was the impetus to try another. Familiar with the classic children's literature her parents had read her, she believed *Winnie-the-Pooh* would be a good subject for a coloring book. "I've always loved *Winnie-the-Pooh*. Really loved him with a *passion*, you know? Before Disney or anyone else got hold of it. . . ."

Boucher called the publisher of the *Pooh* series. "I found they did not own the merchandising rights and they classified coloring books as merchandise." She adds that since her success they've changed their minds. *"Everybody* changed their minds."

A woman, Shirley Schlesinger, had inherited the *Pooh* rights from her dead husband, who had bought them from A. A. Milne. Connie Boucher flew to New York to meet with Mrs. Schlesinger. In retrospect, Connie says of her actions, "Crazy, crazy." What did her friends and family think as she flew to New York with this seemingly wild scheme? "They thought I was nuts!" The women met over lunch. Schlesinger's comment: "Coloring book!" There was little or no *Pooh* merchandise at that time, and Boucher explains that Schlesinger "really didn't understand it. No one did. And I bought the rights for five hundred dollars. And that started the whole thing."

Boucher smiles and is silent, for once. Young, whose voice is usually obliterated by Boucher's enthusiastic storytelling, states, "She just did it."

Young "kicked" the coloring book cover up to an unheard-of 15" × 18" size, and the original illustrations and text from the *Pooh* books were reproduced. The cover had a black background printed with white ink. An innovative look.

"Wait until you hear how we printed the first book! I mortgaged the house! The collateral was the house!" As she calms down, Boucher explains, "We were going to print two thousand pieces." Yet she had no orders and the printer's charge was about fifteen hundred dollars. "He said, 'Well, what do you have?' 'A mortgaged house.'" The printer printed; he felt she would be responsible. "So really it was like talking everybody into everything. Credit, the whole thing!" Her voice becomes quiet for emphasis. The printer loved the concept, according to Boucher.

Friends and acquaintances started to comment on the fledgling

entrepreneur's efforts: "What do you know about any of it?"
Boucher explains you don't *have* to know anything about it. You
simply go and do it.

She says she thinks book dealers carried her coloring books
because "in the first place some people felt really sorry and thought
I was going to cry or something. I really did look that way. 'We'll
take two,' they would say, and they'd call back right away and say,
'I'll take six more of those.'" Boucher's voice, filled with self-awe,
is almost a whisper. (In a 1966 *Newsweek* article, "Women at the
Top," Boucher talked about this starting period of her business:
"They think, 'Oh boy, this dizzy blonde is really going to need all
the help that she can get.'")

She started without an office. "I had papers down the hall, all
over the bed, into a little den. . . . 'Okay,' I said, 'we're going to
get started. One of us has got to not work,'" and she resigned
from her Magnin's position.

Connie no longer brought home a paycheck, yet the Bouchers
found they were able to pay their bills with Determined Productions profits. She said to herself, "Gee, this is fun and you can
make money as well, you know?" She continued personally to
market the books. "I did all the selling and I sold it all the way
across the country." She was at the printer every morning at eight
o'clock with the orders that were typed the night before. Although
Jim Young and John Boucher owned a part of the company,
Connie says she was doing the labor. "Yeah." She reconsiders.
"But they were all working. John was writing copy. And, you
know, we printed two thousand pieces and I took them to the
stores and sold them and in the next six months we had two
twenty-five-thousand reprints. They were three dollars retail and
they had never had a book this size." The company netted 75¢
each; 52,000 times 75¢ equals almost $40,000.

As sales escalated, Determined Productions rented a room in

an old building. James Young came after work, and Boucher laughs as she remembers: "John quit his [regular] job very fast. . . . Once you start something, that's great. But to sustain it is the problem with most people. John thought it was fun at first," but later lost interest. James Young and Connie Boucher often worked alone together.

A total of twelve giant coloring books were marketed; Boucher says they were almost too nice to give to children. They did *Pooh*, *The Wonderful Wizard of Oz*, *Alice's Adventures in Wonderland*, *The Wind in the Willows*—all from the original illustrations. "The covers were very graphic. The whole series is marvelous." A *Raggedy Ann and Andy* coloring book was eventually added, as well as *Babar*, with both French and English captions.

Boucher needed a better distribution system than the one she was personally handling, so a national plan was set up. She checked a book that lists salespeople who handle specific products on a commission basis, and, she says, "I picked [names and addresses] out of that list and just sent letters to the first ten people in different areas," with a sample, asking if they would handle the coloring books. One salesman remembers thinking as he received Boucher's letter, "Who is this crazy nut? I thought everything was wrong, the wrong size. . . . Tell me why I said yes. I don't know." Boucher says, "Oddly enough, on that list there were two women, so I got two saleswomen right away. . . . They are *tremendous!*" Eight national salespeople finally sold her wares.

Distribution grew almost by itself. When your company name is on a product and the item sells, according to Boucher, people start coming to you.

Boucher worked on her own publicity and public relations. She and her two growing boys colored the pages in the *Pooh* coloring book, pasting them on walls as wallpaper, and Boucher sent a photo of the room to *Look* magazine. An editor called her.

"He liked *Pooh*," says Boucher. *Look* did a wall themselves, took a "smashing picture," and it was published. "That was our first publicity thing." So she thought, If *Look* went for it, maybe *Life* will, too. The weekly was doing a series titled *"Life* Goes to a Party." Boucher thought, What about *"Life* Goes to a Pooh Party"? *Life* magazine's reaction: "What's a Pooh party?"

Connie Boucher showed them what a Pooh party was. On a tract of land, she built Pooh's house in a tree. "It was all fun, you know?" Someone fell out of the tree during the building; they held barbecues while construction work was going on. *Life* did three pages of *"Life* Goes to a Pooh Party." The Bouchers' son Teddy and his friends were the guests. "And we had Eeyore's house . . . and Owl's house in the tree and Pooh's house in this big old burnt-up huge redwood kind of a thing, so it was really so authentic that it was amazing." Boucher, whose voice becomes hushed, recalls these happenings.

In the 1960s there was little of this sort of "character" merchandise. There were Raggedy Ann dolls and articles tying into them, a Shirley Temple doll, Hopalong Cassidy items, Daniel Boone coonskin hats, a Batman doll. Most Mickey Mouse items evolved later, with Disneyland. The few products on the market did not cover a wide range. Boucher had an idea.

When an employee in Boucher's New York sales office was asked if Charles Schulz's Snoopy made Determined Productions successful, she said, "No, *Connie* made *Snoopy* the big thing." Boucher—who says Schulz is a genius—cringes at such talk. Whatever, Charles Schulz's *Peanuts* characters and Constance Boucher's Determined Productions helped each other.

Boucher, a fan of Charles Schulz's, describes the events leading up to her producing *Peanuts* merchandise: "First of all, what I did was send Sparky [Schulz] a coloring book. A *Winnie-the-Pooh*, and of course he knew *Winnie-the-Pooh*. Then I called him. He answered his own telephone at that time. So he said, 'What is this all about?' and I explained." She proposed a date book, a calendar. A novel item. He directed her to call United Features Syndicate, owners of the Charles Schulz characters and strip. Boucher continues: "So I went to New York and met the man who was in charge of merchandising [at United Features Syndicate]. At that time there wasn't any merchandise. So I told him what we wanted to do. . . . I don't think we paid for it. I don't think it cost anything at all. . . . not any up-front money. Just a royalty deal and if it worked, it did." James Young's analysis: United Features Syndicate took one look at Boucher and decided she would never get it off the ground. If in fact the U.F.S. executive did have that reaction, he was dead wrong.

Boucher's decision to focus on the *Peanuts* characters— designing, manufacturing, wholesaling, and/or licensing, de- pending upon the product—was perhaps profound: lacking any age barrier, appealing to both sexes, and clearly nonpolitical, it was an essentially neuter—in other words, highly marketable— product. And the dollar value to Boucher's firm is phenomenal. The majority of articles relating to the *Peanuts* characters are Determined Productions items. According to vice-president Young, if you think you often see Determined products in the United States, "you should see them in Japan. Snoopy is very big in Japan. They sell as many plush Snoopys in Japan as they do here." Quips Boucher, "Snoopy's Japanese, I'm sure, by now. . . . It's huge. It's amazing."

Connie's corporation made millions on Schulz's *Peanuts* characters before branching into other licensed products. Her personal life was not as smooth-running. As Determined Pro- ductions kept doubling their sales, Constance Boucher's marriage continued to fall apart. "I've known her for twenty-three years, and it's interesting to me the breaks she's had to make psychologically to get to where she is," comments a friend. The most significant was away from her husband, John.

When discussing her divorce, she says, "Our father was a very bright, warm, unbelievable human being," and the problem with her marriage was her unrealistic expectations. She thought she was marrying a man who was like her father. Later she decided such people are rare. She turns wistfully to her mother and says, "We were so naïve, Evie." Referring to the marriage expectations that she and her sister had, and their subsequent divorces.

Eve Klingsborg insists her sons-in-law were "very nice boys. We got along well." John Boucher was a quiet man, quieter than the vivacious, talkative Connie, who says: "In a group he was always pretty good. I found that as time went along he got very dull. . . . I wanted to do a lot of things, I wanted to go to a lot of places, and I wanted to fly around the world and I wanted to get on with things [referring no doubt to the business of making money], and I was too much. I was impossible."

When the marriage ended in the late sixties, Connie bought her ex-husband's share of Determined Productions. He then retired. Present owners in addition to the president are sons Douglas and Theodore . . . and James Young. Young and Boucher live together.

One of the rare times Boucher did not have a ready answer was when she was asked when she and Young became emotionally involved. A long pause. "I don't know." Connie adds quickly, filling in the silence: "Actually not early in our relationship. . . . We worked together, we did a lot of things together, but we really did not get romantically involved until after I got divorced. Oddly. Really a funny situation. Because everybody thought it was otherwise. [She warms to the subject.] And it absolutely was not, which is *almost* crazy . . . it was really an unusual relationship." They have been together almost ten years.

Emotionally compatible, Jim Young and Connie Boucher function as a team. He is art director; she clearly gives orders and speaks like the boss. Together they represent the success of Determined, whose products include the plush Snoopy, a stuffed animal manufactured in several sizes. A double for Schulz's sketch, the toy won an M.I.T. design award as an excellent embodiment of a one-dimensional drawing and, according to Boucher and Young, great pains are taken to insure high-quality materials and workmanship. Determined produces out-fits for the stuffed dog—Snoopy the rock star (with blue star-shaped "shades"), the doctor (with a green surgical mask placed over his snout), beagle-scout, train engineer, flying ace, hippie (denim jacket and pants with tail hole). Says Boucher, "We're making a pair of Dr. Denton's [footed pajamas] for Snoopy right now with the feet in them, you know? Can you believe it?"

Like the plush Snoopy, many products are designed and actu-ally manufactured by Determined Productions; others are cooperative ventures where licensed corporations create, design, and merchandise, and at times use their own corporate name on the product. The final look comes from Determined Pro-ductions, however. And the character drawing is always a Schulz design. For example, when Determined Productions and Danskin designed a Snoopy dress together, the actual Snoopy lying on his back was from Schulz's pen.

J. P. Stevens manufactures *Peanuts* bedding. Remember, when you see Snoopy (with few exceptions), Determined is mak-ing money. An employee says that in one year, the Stevens's *Peanuts* line grossed ten million dollars, "the single biggest-selling sheet pattern ever produced in the history of the domestics industry."

Determined has rights for all children's and women's ready-to-wear products. In collaboration with Determined Productions,

Cartier is designing a solid-gold Snoopy, with platinum also under consideration. With a diamond nose. And perhaps sterling-silver Snoopy pillboxes—miniature doghouses with an opening roof.

Ninety million readers follow the *Peanuts* strip; Boucher's rights are worth a fortune. A Determined employee explains the setup: "United Features Syndicate in essence owns Mr. Schulz. Owns the *Peanuts* characters... because Mr. Schulz came to them twenty-seven years ago and asked them to distribute his comic strip. They have merchandise rights, which they have given to certain people, and Determined Productions has the majority of these rights. Hallmark has the greeting cards, stationery, gift wrap—those kinds of paper products and a few little odds and ends. Between Determined Productions and Hallmark are... about 85 percent to 90 percent of the rights."

Connie Boucher and friends

In addition to *Peanuts* products, Boucher's company produces Joan Walsh Anglund character merchandise and is considering *Wizard of Oz* dolls. Connie laments, "We just haven't had time." Susan Perl characters (seen in Health-Tex ads) are a Determined property; Boucher's firm places the various characters on watches, sleeping bags, Christmas ornaments, books.

And this is not enough for the spunky Boucher. "We've got ten new directions we want to go in," she states. Open a restaurant. Produce a movie. Get into television. She is working on a group of nonlicensed items which are Determined's own creations. Her office is alive with ideas.

Determined Productions is located in a former San Francisco factory. The office is cheerfully and stylishly decorated in primary greens and reds, with blue carpeting, pure white walls and globe light fixtures. White inverted schoolroom-style shades cover the floor-to-ceiling front windows to the left of the item-display area. Lush potted plants—in smooth white containers—abound. Within the essentially one-room corporate headquarters is a people-sized doghouse, with display shelves packed with products for buyers to view. This concept was also adapted to retail setups. Snoopy doghouse boutiques displaying *Peanuts* merchandise were placed in department stores after Boucher wrote to store presidents across the country and asked them to get into the doghouse with Determined. Most of them did.

Near the doghouse display but hidden within an ell sits Connie Boucher, her back to the wall. Far across the room is "Son of Founder," as Douglas Boucher refers to himself. Eve Klingsborg and June Klingsborg Dutton sit between the two Bouchers. All three desks face the boss, rather like a royal court with the throne at the head. Beyond them are a glass-walled computer center and, through a corridor, Jim Young's art department.

In her corner Connie is surrounded by artwork celebrating the nude figure. A full-sized statue of a nude woman pulling a dress over her head stands on the floor with a three-dimensional wall hanging of women's midriffs close by. Another female nude sculpture is on her desk, plus a sculptured pair of thighs. Next to her phone, a male torso, a gilt Chinese puzzle of nudes, a wooden nude torso on a wooden pedestal, and an abstract couple (male-female? female-female?), plus a clay nude woman pulling on a strand of her hair. A nude sculpture behind her chair, and one at the side, as well as another in front of her work area. They keep a visitor busy as Connie runs to confer or handles long-distance telephone calls. A sculpted set of legs nearby, she explains, is entitled "London Knees." "I'd love to have a collection of male torsos. . . . I'd love to have 'David.' I would have male sculptures if they were available. They don't do males as frequently as they do females. Why don't they do more men? Tell me? But men have gorgeous bodies. Yes. Sure."

Boucher's nudes blend with every size and kind of ceramic and stuffed Snoopy; a humanlike mutt stares from every niche and corner. And velveteen Woodstocks and Peppermint Pattys. Says June Dutton, "It's usually the new employees" who have them sitting on their desks.

In the back art rooms, art director Young is designing a Snoopy toothpaste container. Snoopy toothpaste? "Oh, yeah. You name it," says June. Everyone is busy, phones ringing, employees scurrying.

Boucher does not reveal yearly sales, yet admits published figures are "always way behind." A financial reporting service credits Determined Productions with twenty million dollars in annual sales. The president smiles and says, "We are in good shape."

In addition to the United States office, there is a Hong Kong company, branches in Tokyo, and a Swedish sales company, with distributors throughout the world. With fourteen thousand

The Klingsborg connection—Evie Klingsborg, Kit Dutton, Connie Boucher, Lisa Dutton, Douglas Boucher

regularly active solid accounts, Boucher comments, "We've really developed in the past ten years."

When Boucher discusses and describes her enterprise, she is simple, straightforward. The basic common sense pervades and that incredible drive is evident. Women are their own worst enemy, she says, and—amazing to her—do not realize their worth. "First they have to look at themselves and believe in themselves." Boucher thinks a lot of American females could become successful with encouragement. An example of the degree of success attainable, she is an optimist and, her mother says, "jumps into anything she does with both feet, believes nothing is impossible." Boucher's round face becomes animated as she speaks encouraging words to women: "I know we're mothers, and we copy our mothers, but if you can do that [conquer the job of motherhood by imitation] you can do the other. . . . And I wonder why more women don't take that other step. I know it takes more energy and it takes more time. . . ." It takes a Constance Klingsborg Boucher. Women can get to the same position as men but, she feels, they sometimes must do things differently. "You don't just get anywhere by attack. It's just like with little kids. . . ." She believes in kidding the males along, and finds men from a liberal household, where "Mommie and Daddy were equal," are better employees, easier to deal with at a business level. When Boucher goes to Japan, according to Young, she is told a woman does not conduct business as in the United States. "But Connie doesn't pay any attention," he says. Her feeling is "They're businessmen, shrewd as the next guy," and if she brings business, they talk to her.

Boucher thinks and moves quickly. James Young describes their life together as hectic. He discusses their personally preparing three hundred tamales for a coming party between business jaunts from Hong Kong to Europe, at the same time packing business-connected items in a dozen cartons, running the regular business, and remodeling the ground floor of their house. Young, in his quiet slow voice, muses slowly: "Every minute, every hour, and then she decides that. . ."

"*What?*" exclaims Connie loudly, impatient for the punch line.

Young finishes his thought: ". . . every night she has to invite somebody for dinner because she doesn't have enough to do. And then after dinner she has to go through more papers, more papers. . . ."

Boucher, who interjects "Exactly" and "Yep" into her conversations regularly, refers to "we" and "us" when she talks about business, sharing the glory with Young. Jim speaks so rarely it's hard to determine how he refers to Determined Productions. When he does comment, she is likely to interrupt him. Sometimes Jim starts a sentence when Connie is still jabbering— perhaps in self-defense. They at times attempt to—and do—speak simultaneously. But Connie's voice takes over, and Jim becomes quiet. Although she often asks Young questions to draw him into a conversation, she does not necessarily wait for his answer. Even when her mouth is full of cherries, she manages to converse 99 percent of the time while Young sits by with a rather innocent smile.

Looks are deceiving. Beneath this soft friendly exterior lurk strength of purpose, artistic talent, and appreciation and love for Boucher. Huge, tall, and broad, he likes to dress in all black. In his dark turtleneck and black corduroy suit, he is always in the background, commenting softly, occasionally.

She and Young work well together. Her comment: "Um-huh. Yeah. We do. Um-huh. He can stand this kind of woman." He is a great deal like her father. "When they say girls fall in love with their fathers, maybe they're not so far off, huh?"

Boucher and Young reside in a San Francisco Victorian mansion—along with her pairs of shoes. This childhood love continues: "I love shoes. God, I *love* shoes. I'm *crazy* about shoes. I like shoes and boots. I travel with five pairs of boots!" And she buys some she never wears. She is fond of—and it gives her a certain special kind of style—large silver jewelry. "I love silver. I *love* silver."

In contrast to sister June's observation about her being a sloppy child, Boucher is neat today: "I'm very classified." When working on many different subjects, she cannot come back later to straighten papers. "There is no doing that." So she places items where they belong immediately.

Organized, affectionate, loyal, Boucher still works with individuals she did business with years ago, including her original printer; these associates are almost an extended family. Manufacturers, retail buyers, distributors.

Boucher considers her family-run company an ideal corporation. The warmth and closeness exemplified by this Klingsborg clan is unusual. Her son Ted, rebel of the family and fugitive from the business (Connie says he's the oldest hippie she knows), lives in the California countryside and sees Determined as a "total rat race." Her older son, Douglas, views Determined differently. He had some disquieting years before joining the business. "All that turmoil built character. Without it, what are you?" he says, and, after quipping he is "Son of Founder," adds "I'm vice-president. I do a lot of administrative work."

Connie and Young are overseas frequently while her son manages the United States interests. He is rarely involved in the creative aspects. His brother Ted is the artistic one.

Douglas, a short, well-built, lean man, remembers his and his brother's childhood: "I was a 'yesman' as a child." His cynicism becomes perhaps pedantic and somewhat overdone. Yet his personable mother is tough competition. After claiming Connie is a tyrant, he says seriously she was a strict but fair disciplinarian and today they usually agree, Young: "You should see them go at each other around here." Everyone concurs that Connie has a temper and yells when she's angry, but Douglas qualifies that when he was growing up, she was not a spanker. "I don't think her drive takes her in that direction." Is your mother a logical-thinking individual? "At times, yeah." Young agrees, "At times." Connie interjects, "That means 'Not always,' guys. Say it!" Douglas Boucher elaborates: "Lots of times her gut reactions to situations I think are not necessarily thought out on logical terms, but the decisions are very logical if you analyze them. Do you know what I mean? Well, they're more intuitive. . . . But they work." Young adds that Connie Boucher thinks in a rather indirect manner, as he moves his hands in the air to explain graphically. "She doesn't go like this," and he puts his hands straight ahead of him. (She loves his act.) "I don't think even *she* knows where she is intending to go," states Young, who finds it maddening. "But she knows there's something over there that has to be reached." Boucher, June, Doug, and Eve laugh.

A family business. Boucher's mother—"Everybody calls me Evie"—loves being involved with Determined. "I won't quit until I can't navigate. I walk to work every day; it's a good mile." Eve is the company proofreader. Boucher says, "She writes the best letters in this place. She picks up stuff that people have overlooked," and handles complaints with a diplomatic touch.

The business-personal relationship between Connie Boucher and Evie is special. When Mrs. Klingsborg talks about being a "lucky-lucky" person born on Friday the thirteenth—a remark her daughter must have heard dozens of times—Connie laughs with delight at her mother's clever light humor. These women like, love, and respect one another. When Mrs. Klingsborg says her parents were married on Friday the thirteenth as well, Connie's sincere response is "Well, that was good luck for all of us, Evie."

June Dutton is different from her older sister. Their mother feels that June, once the society editor of the San Mateo *Times*, is the more academic of the two; Connie is a doer and Dutton is probably more philosophical. "They're both gregarious," she adds. Dutton writes the company's ethnic and geographic square, paperback cookbooks, another Determined product. When Connie Boucher is traveling and her vice-president son is away, "I'm the next in line," says June.

June's son is in production and her daughter works in the art department. There is another cousin by marriage involved in the company. A total of eight—including James Young—make up the Klingsborg connection, the strength of Determined Productions.

But the source of life and spirit behind the Klingsborgs is the woman who as a little girl managed to coerce a tarnished dime away from her sister, trading her own shiny penny. Says June, "Right there, that's it."

5

A PREGNANT PATTERN

Edna Ravkind and Elsie Frankfurt Pollock

———————··⟨∞⟩··———————

... SHE SITS in the dappled shadow of a slowly swaying euca-
lyptus tree near blossoms, red, blue, pink, yellow, reflecting in the
swimming pool beside her. Elsie Frankfurt Pollock—her perfectly groomed figure resembling that measure of perfection, the
hourglass—speaks in a gravelly voice overlaid with soothing
Texan tones about the beginnings of her maternity-wear company. . . .

Elsie Frankfurt, in 1938 a Southern Methodist University
graduate, never held a job and had no idea what profession she
wished to pursue.

Adept at sewing, the new graduate offered to make her twenty-
three-year-old expectant sister, Edna, a frock.

Edna Ravkind, in a chic suède suit, walks along a Dallas sidewalk toward her and Elsie's corporate building. "Good morning, Mrs. Ravkind," an employee with a Texas drawl greets her. Edna smiles absent-mindedly and passes by into her private office.

Elsie designed a new outfit for her older sister "because she looked so terrible in some dresses of Mama's that were too big for her." Before World War II, pregnant women's fashion choices were clothes several sizes larger than normal, or else Hooverettes, a kind of a wraparound affair. These enlarged attires allowed room for the full tummy but hung loosely off the wearers' shoulders and generally had no shape. So Elsie designed what ultimately was the first Page Boy dress, "and Edna looked like a human being again." Elsie quips, "Instead of going over the obstacle, I went around it." She realized her sister would look more fashionable with a hole cut in the front of the skirt material, allowing the abdomen room, yet with the rest of the skirt still fitting the hips and derrière. This was before modern-day stretch fabrics, which today round out the problem. To cover the open area in the skirt front, Elsie Frankfurt designed a smock top, whose hemline hung below the cutout, and a jacket.

. . . Elsie Frankfurt Pollock leans forward and her soft eyes brighten as she reminisces in the endless summer of her Holmby Hills home; other residents of this Los Angeles neighborhood include Glen Campbell, Rod Stewart, Henry Mancini, Eva Gabor, Irene Dunne, Betsy Bloomingdale, Cher, Edgar Bergen. Around the corner from the pool, her lush grounds contain a tennis court. She relaxes nearby as her white-jacketed houseman serves freshly squeezed strawberry juice in oversized goblets. With the sun glistening on her blond hair, Elsie Pollock, president of Page Boy Maternity Fashions, epitomizes the beautiful

Californian. "I'm thinking now," she says. "It's all coming back. . . ." More than thirty years ago . . .

Expectant women continually asked Edna Frankfurt Ravkind where they might purchase an outfit like hers, and were so persistent that Elsie and Edna opened a shop in their home town of Dallas and began manufacturing and selling Elsie's invention—the maternity dress.

"We had five hundred dollars between us, my sister and I." Their first shop, "about the size of that little corner over there"—she points to an area to the left of her pool where a variety of tropical plants, flawlessly pruned, grow in profusion—"with one little dressing room. We didn't tell our father anything about it."

The store was located in the same building as was their father's physician, whom Mr. Frankfurt visited one day, and the following conversation ensued:

Doctor: "What do you think about the girls going into business?"

Father: "*What* business?"

Mr. Frankfurt ran downstairs, and there they were. Elsie and Edna. "We were opened," recalls Elsie, delighted.

Elsie Pollock has a highly developed sense of humor. She relates her father's comment that the newly formed business reminded him of the man who says he's in the lumber business and sells matches. This is followed by her heavy laughter. "That was his whole attitude." More chuckling. "Mama knew all along. Oh, sure, she was right in the middle of it."

The rent in that first shop, with its tiny workroom in the back, was thirty-five dollars a month; one style frock in a variety of fabrics was sold. Two women were hired to sew and the five hundred dollars in savings covered the seamstresses' salaries until the women realized a profit. Furniture was bought at a state fair for about a hundred dollars. "A couple of rattan little chairs and things..." The mayor's wife was one of their first customers. "*That* I remember." In a short time, the two sisters were able to pay themselves salaries, and their younger sister, Louise (always called "Tootsie"), joined the enterprise when she finished college.

A fine specialty store in Atlanta wired the Frankfurt sisters after seeing their dress on a customer visiting from Texas. The retail store asked if Page Boy wholesaled the dresses. "We wired back immediately, 'Of course.' So they ordered six dresses." Elsie says kiddingly, "We had our big workroom make up six dresses."

Within six months they netted three thousand dollars.

When a friend offered to take their dress to New York to try and sell it, Elsie said, "Why not?" So everybody said, "What'll you do if she sells the dresses?" She did. The dress sold for $22.95 retail. "It was a lot; twelve dollars and seventy-five cents wholesale." She calculates it would retail for fifty dollars today. "At least."

Customers bought the frock in all colors. "That's all they would wear." Another standard Elsie statement: "I never wanted to be the biggest. I just wanted to be the best. We were on the level where I wanted. We weren't catering to the masses." (In Dallas, one of Edna Ravkind's staff says, "We start at twenty-seven dollars on up for a dress," with the tops starting at fifteen dollars and going to about fifty dollars. "People will pay for our label.")

Elsie recalls: "We're sitting down in Dallas now with all these orders...." Other Manhattan stores also wanted the dress. A Chicago firm ordered a hundred pieces. "I remember the day." The retailer got the hundred in, sold them, and immediately reordered another hundred. "We were made." As the business started to mushroom, Elsie Frankfurt did not say to herself, "This little project is going to make a lot of money." She says now, "I didn't have time to think."

The dresses—bearing the Page Boy label with the logo of a little page boy with a trumpet ("That was my thought," Elsie says; it was a boy announcing the arrival of the heir to the throne)— were moving so well that she and Edna hired a forelady and a part-time cutter. "And we were really in business."

The only time Page Boy used borrowed cash, Elsie says, was

A 1964 yoga break at Page Boy with Elsie *(center)* and Edna *(right)*

between shipping those first large orders "until the time they paid 8/10, E.O.M. We were running a little short." Mr. Frankfurt co-signed a note for three thousand dollars at the bank; he had finally come around to thinking that the business was going to be successful. The loan was paid off within two months. "And to this day we never borrowed again," says Elsie.

In Texas, Edna Frankfurt Ravkind—a five-foot-three-inch, slender (weight 116 pounds), brown-eyed, gray-haired fashion plate—sits in her black, white, and mirrored office and, in her high Texas-accented voice, recalls that manufacturing was just organized when she and her mother took a vacation trip to California. She spotted a shop across from Bullock's-Wilshire in Los Angeles and called Elsie to say she thought they should open a store there: "I found the perfect spot for it." In the middle of setting up a large-scale manufacturing and while machinery was being delivered and installed, it seemed rather overambitious. Elsie was home with her father, who was yelling, "Don't crawl before you walk!" Their mother, in California, was all for it. Edna signed a lease and opened the first California Page Boy outlet.

Volume increased although there were problems.

When, during World War II, Elsie went to New York City to buy fabric, she recalls, "My sister would say it was better for me not to go, because I wouldn't pay the price." She adds, "You know what goes on in our world." But did she get the fabric? Without paying the price? "Well, I got enough. We managed."

The two sisters, with Tootsie (a long-time staffer states this sister—no longer associated with the firm—is the "sweetest of the three girls"), worked well together. Tootsie Frankfurt Gartner had employees work for days to insure a perfect fit. Based upon her own figure. Was she a perfect size? "No," says a veteran Page Boy

worker. A perfectionist, Tootsie was creative and had artistic ability. But she left Page Boy as her children occupied more of her
time. According to an acquaintance of the three Frankfurt sisters,
she reacts the same as the other two: "If she likes you, she can be
wonderful. If not, look out." Edna, in addition to bearing three
children, manufactured and also designed their patented maternity skirt—and eventually a full line of clothing for pregnant
women—while Elsie concentrated on finance, sales, and public
relations.

Life began for these sisters in Dallas, Texas. The family of four
children—Edna, followed by Elsie, and then a brother (who died
at twenty), and the youngest, Tootsie—had an immigrant father,
who came to this country as a boy from Russia; an uncle spon-
sored his entry into the United States. His middle daughter, who
has his sense of humor, remembers his remarking, "It's hell to get
old." He then turned to her, a young woman; "Isn't it, Elsie?"
She laughs heartily at this remembrance of their father, a self-
made man fluent in five languages, who died in 1947. She says,
"I was sort of an oddball. Not the oldest, not the youngest, not
the son. But I think I was Papa's favorite. He thought I was more
like him than any of the others. . . . I was quick. He thought I had
a sharp mind. He had a very sharp mind." She believes her
siblings realized that she was the favored child.

*In her Dallas executive offices, Edna Ravkind, in her faltering
speech pattern, says she thinks that's true: "I really do. Elsie looks
like him. They're very . . . they watch money. Very methodical. He
was . . . what's the word? Tight . . . My father was the head of the
family . . . a brilliant, brilliant man. But I think my mother
would have been the one to make all the money. She was practical. My mother had a very clear head."*

The sisters had a warm and close relationship with their mother, Annie Bergman Frankfurt, right up to her recent death. The parents—although not emotionally demonstrative—created a solid happy Jewish home life for their children. Edna and Tootsie married; Elsie continued to live at home, often traveling to her New York City apartment in the Hotel Pierre or to California to oversee Page Boy interests on the West Coast. After Mr. Frankfurt's death, Elsie occasionally took her mother on business trips.

. . . Elsie Pollock bends her neck as the California sun fully catches her unlined face, and she comments on her surroundings: "This is lovely, isn't it?" With Texan hospitality, she adds, "Make yourself at home!" (When she is asked a question, Elsie Pollock thinks for many seconds; sitting still or with very little movement, she considers the question carefully and the answer. Sometimes she does not respond. She is soft and quiet and often acknowledges with only a gentle nod of the head or even a gesture with her eyes. Being in her presence is a restful experience.) "I'm usually fairly well low-keyed."

In 1949, Elsie decided a Page Boy fashion show should be held, appropriately, in New York's Stork Club. "It was the only place that I wanted." She hired a top commentator, actress Adrienne Ames, and the press covered it. "It was absolutely gorgeous. And that is when we so-called [a favorite expression] broke through and started selling stores like Lord & Taylor." Maternity shorts were introduced for the first time.

With business throughout the United States, Elsie had become corporate president and her business associations were with men; she continued to reside with her mother in Dallas. "We had a

Elsie Frankfurt with model at 1958 fashion show

very nice relationship, and I was too busy in the business and couldn't see any reason to have my own apartment."

Although a friend observed that Elsie did not need a lover because she had Page Boy, she dated frequently. And she became, as she says, "very tired arguing. 'Why won't you have an affair with me? Why? Why? Why?' I kept saying, 'Well if you like me the way I am, I am the way I am, and that's it.'"

And that was it until she met Frank Pollock. In 1966, after decades as a bachelor woman and company president, Elsie Frankfurt wed Pollock. Why did she wait to marry? "I always talked myself out of it. . . . I could always think of more reasons why not than why. If you give me enough time, I can talk myself out of anything. Frank, thank goodness, didn't give me any time to think."

Elsie considers the courtship the romance of the century— "Well, as far as I'm concerned!"—and enjoys relating her personal love story. Finishing her work in Boston—there had been a fashion show at Jordan Marsh and other fine stores—she stopped in New York before flying home. A friend called imploring her to join a dinner party; there was a man for Elsie to meet. Frankfurt already had a date and was preparing at that moment to go out. "You know," she says, "you meet so many. You can imagine how many blind dates... You think you never want to have another blind date anyway. But you know, like the firemen, the bell rings, you go to the fire." Her friend urged her and her date to stop by after their meal for an after-dinner drink. She agreed. At the apartment, following introductions and general conversing, she recalls, "Frank came over to me and he said (he's very slow), 'Are you all tied up?' I said, 'No.' He said, 'Well, when can I see you?' Very coyly I said, 'When would you like to see me?'" He asked her out for the next night but she was busy. They fixed an appointment for Friday. Over a decade later, Elsie remembers the days of the week each episode of the courtship occurred.

Amazingly, so does Frank. "This was on Wednesday. And then Thursday he called. . . . Then the flowers started coming. For the next few weeks. And he doesn't send a little bouquet, I can tell you." On their first evening together he told her he had four ex-wives. And a forty-year-old son. And two little children at home. "And I thought, Another wasted evening, Elsie. . . . You've got to expect a bad one every so often."

He was a charmer that night, Elsie recalls. Very direct. They went to El Morocco—"Those were the days one still went to El Morocco"—where he looked at her and said, "I'm going to marry you." And she thought, Honey, *who needs you!*

That was Friday night. "On Saturday he said 'How about coming up to the country?'" Frank Pollock owned a Westchester County estate—his children were with their mother for the weekend—and she agreed to go if he could have her back in the city for a date that evening. (Today Frank wonders if she really did have plans for that night.) At the end of the lovely spring day at his Hudson River home, he asked her to come again the next day. She agreed.

"And it was beautiful," she remembers. At one point he suggested she call her mother in Dallas. Why not? Free telephone call, thought Elsie as she dialed: "'Mom, how are you? . . . Fine.' Then he gets on the phone. And he says, 'I'm going to marry your daughter.' Mama, God bless her, said, 'If Elsie's happy, then I'm happy. . . .' She thought he was someone else!"

Elsie tells this story for an hour. Every fact is indelibly etched in her memory. It's obvious she is thrilled by the tale. Her Romeo. "Every day, the flowers would come. Every day, what did I want to do? He sent all kinds of flowers. All in boxes. I wish he had sent them arranged, because I'll tell you, I was calling and calling for more vases and more vases. Oh, he turns a hell of a campaign." He had a dinner party for her. And his close friends, the Seagram's Bronfmans, held a luncheon; another couple had a dinner in her honor. Frank suggested they look for a ring: "Dennis [Frank's chauffeur] picked me up on Broadway where our office was, and Frank walked over from his office in the Seagram Building. [Pollock manufactures bottles of the type liquor is sold in.] It's just like you see in the picture show. They [at Van Cleef's] bring out the trays. . . . I never would buy jewelry for myself. I always had a feeling it should be given with love. Because to me it's a beautiful way of expressing love."

On to Harry Winston, Cartier, Tiffany. . . . By now the couple had known each other two weeks. Before she left for Dallas, a flawless ten-carat canary-yellow diamond was on her finger. It was her first engagement. She wonders what he would have done if she'd chosen one of the really big stones.

According to Elsie, Frank Pollock was "coming on like gang-busters" when she walked into one of her shops and an employee recommended she draw a Dun & Bradstreet rating on him. Elsie thought it was an incredible idea; she did nothing about it. Elsie remembers Frank saying later that same day over dinner, " 'Say, what happened to that two hundred thousand dollars between this year and last year?' He had drawn a D. & B. on *me!*" His comment: "Well, I didn't want a girl who was going to be marrying me for my money." They both find this whole incident absolutely hilarious.

Frank borrowed a London town house from friends and announced they were to be there for a July honeymoon. She said, "There's no way I can possibly be ready by July. I'm running a business. . . ." But he didn't give her time to think. According to him, the children would not be a difficulty; her business would be no problem. With her two sisters in Dallas, she could continue as Page Boy's president while living in the Northeast.

Frank Pollock and his bride married at the Hotel Pierre. One gift sits on their piano, a sterling Cinderella carriage from Cartier, which arrived with a note stating, "She finally found her Prince Charming." Precisely how she views the union.

"I don't think I was ever in love before Frank. They all seem to fade. . . ." She had never lived with a man or traveled, as a couple, with a male. "There were so many who did want to sleep with me, as you know. Maybe that was another thing in Frank's favor. He didn't even ask. . . . All I can tell you is I told him he took an awful chance!" She mentions he bought the package without unwrapping it. "That's not his past history." Perhaps it was the smartest deal he ever managed.

Her 1966 marriage suddenly placed her in the traditional female slot within a family setting. Overseer of a live-in couple, chauffeur, chauffeur's wife, governess, laundress, gardeners. Wife, and mother to an eight-year-old and a ten-year-old: "It had to be run as a children-oriented house and not as an adult house. It was a going business. It was their house I had moved into. And I made it work. In retrospect, I really don't know how I did it. I'd been in business all my life, had never married, and when I did marry Frank, with two children at home, all my friends thought, My goodness, what is going to happen to Elsie? You know, after all these years of independence. . . ." A friend's comment: "Virginia [Pollock's third wife and mother of Bobby and Penny, the two children] didn't get the children; Elsie did." She found herself attending morning coffee at the children's private school, involved in her stepdaughter's dancing class, and class mother of the fourth grade. And president of Page Boy.

Little Bobby Pollock and his stepmother immediately formed a firm relationship. But Penny had problems. It took Elsie—with the erratic help of her husband—time and effort to straighten the child out. Frank Pollock comments, "When a mother walks out

Elsie in her wedding gown, 1966

on them, it's a trying experience for two youngsters. And she [Elsie] filled that void. You don't have to ask me what kind of mother she is. She and Penny are perhaps closer than Penny and I are." [Penny, a still-maturing young woman in her early twenties: "I'm very, very, very, very, very close to my father, and at times I think that Elsie is a little jealous."] Says Elsie today, "They realize what I did for them, actually." Robert Pollock, a University of California student, comments softly, "Elsie's an unusual woman. I really do love her."

Elsie remembers a corner in her room she fixed for tea parties. Her stepson would make the beverage, and, she says, "Bobby and I would sit down on the floor with low pillows." When they moved to their California house, Bob, now grown up, set up an area in a room with the original tea china as a surprise for his stepmother.

Tea parties, and jacks. Frank would come home to find his bride on the floor with her legs spread out, and would yell, "What are you doing wasting time playing jacks?" She found this an excellent communication vehicle, however: "All of a sudden barriers are down, because when you're playing jacks you're on the same level. And I could beat both of them like crazy!" She laughs in her low-rough style. According to Frank, Elsie "moved the governess out pretty fast," and tried to be there herself when the children came home from school. Robert Pollock says, "Elsie's there when you really need her."

Mrs. Pollock remembers the more difficult times, as well as the pleasant experiences, as she brought up the two children. An F. A. O. Schwarz Christmas catalogue arrived yearly before, and the Pollock children marked their choices. "And if they checked, that was a direct order to Santa Clause. . . . I didn't change that but I did discipline them." Robert Pollock says the pre-Elsie days included buying whatever he and his sister wished from the

Good Humor man, stocking up the freezer, handing Popsicles out to friends. Elsie put a stop to it. "She made me itemize my purchases. She taught us the value of money." On her penny-pinching ways, he adds, "She overdoes it." And a Page Boy executive comments: "Mrs. Pollock wants an accounting of *every* penny."

Penny Pollock—she speaks with a shaky voice, as if verging on tears—on her stepmother: "She is really a very, very unique person. I have never really met any other woman like her." Elsie came into her life, "when I was like ten, and it was really hard. Very, very bad." Penny's mother had had an affair for five years and her father was not aware of it. (It's hard to believe Frank Pollock would miss a trick.) "My father cannot stand to be alone. Absolutely not." Nine months later, he met Elsie and, although dating "some stupid little actress in New York," he fell in love immediately. At the time Elsie walked into her life, Penny Pollock says she and her brother were "emotionally destroyed."

The marriage between her stepmother and father works because "their interests lie in the same area. And that is business." Robert Pollock comments: "Elsie's 98 percent business, 2 percent domestic." Penny Pollock, who became Mrs. Peter di Grazia in 1978, sees her stepmother as "so realistic it scares you sometimes." Penny, whose positive image of a mother is Elsie, is anxious to be a mother herself: "Elsie has the stature and she projects the satisfaction she has created in her life. Overall she's a really great person and I really, really respect her. In order to love someone, you totally have to respect them. And Elsie fulfills that much more than my mother does. . . ." Does Penny think her father and stepmother will stay together? "Always, absolutely." Her brother Robert says, "Elsie and Dad are very attuned to each other. At night they have dinner, then lie in bed and read annual reports together." Penny describes Elsie as "hard as a brick," while she says her father is a "real strong guy."

Frank Pollock is a dynamic man. In his mid-seventies, he has the vitality of a fifty-year-old. ("I play tennis every day and I swim every day.") Chairman of the board of Thatcher, one of a handful of big glass companies in America, he is, his wife says, "a self-made man. Very self-made. Very made." She giggles. Thatcher merged with Dart Industries—which owns, among other companies, Tupperware—one week before they were married. Elsie mumbles something about two mergers within a seven-day period. Today they live near Dart's corporate headquarters in California. They seem to totally enjoy their elegant existence, and each other.

Question: Does your husband have a nickname for you?

Elsie: "Doll."

Question: What do you call him?

Elsie: "Doll."

Before her marriage, she was interviewed for an article about successful women, and was quoted: "A male executive can marry his secretary, but the successful businesswoman can only make a happy marriage with a man who is eminent in his own right." It took Elsie Frankfurt years to meet the male who could handle her success, drive, energy, and determination. Today she feels she made the right choice in Frank Pollock, who comes across initially as a tough, shrewd individual. With time the impression mellows, but only slightly. Next to her, he seems perhaps coarse.

Ultra-feminine, Mrs. Pollock connects her happiness with Frank to her father. "When you have a very bright father—a man you could look up to—you fall in well with an equally sharp mate." If there is one word to describe Frank Pollock, it is sharp.

Sun-tanned Frank, who has ruddy cheeks and a husky voice, comments on the marriage: "Maybe she told you, maybe she didn't. She's my fifth wife, so I'm a good judge." Loud laughter.

"I'm not going to trade her in. I'm going to keep her." He adds, speaking softly for once, "She's a lovely lady. Of course she's never been married before. She thinks I'm wonderful." His voice gets louder. "So *don't* disillusion her!" He slurs over words, has a rough manner of speech, in direct contrast with his Southern belle, who, he says, has a "beautiful face, lovely figure, and a charming manner. . . . She's quite a girl. She's smart, you know. She has something up there, you know, aside from her good looks. . . . Oh, yeah, she's smart."

Today both say he is in charge around the house. One wonders. He is clearly the louder. He mumbles something about "as long as he signs the checks . . ."

Elsie hardly needs him to pay her bills. Page Boy's retail sales are over five and a half million dollars. He says she is anxious at the end of each business day to know the ten California shops' daily volume: "I think she and her sister are both crazy to carry on this business, you know? Because they've reached an age where they don't have any use for the money any more. Out here [California] we [Page Boy] will do a million and a half dollars, which is a long way from where they were. She talks to her shops on the telephone every day. . . . There's nothing I can do with them. Because this is their pleasure. They don't care for the bridge games and the luncheons." According to Penny, her father believes Elsie—his fragile pure feminine wife—cannot run the business. "Elsie is very cute about it. 'Okay, dear. Yes, dear.'" When Elsie discusses her corporation, she talks about "what I am doing" and "what I did." Frank's discussions concerning Page Boy usually include the plural pronoun "*we,*" as in "We did a lot of business last year."

Frank Pollock is not a man to be in the shadow of his wife. "Never mind all her pictures that she shows you. She didn't show you my pictures, did she?" He presents a framed photograph of himself and Ronald Reagan, and another with Senator Hayakawa.

Elsie says, "Right or wrong, he's always right." Both practically die laughing; they think the same corny jokes are funny, particularly if one of them is the author of such humor.

. . . It is lunchtime in the Pollock household and the houseman begins to serve at the patio table. Elsie stands and gracefully walks toward the umbrella-covered spread; this matured woman is determined to retain the figure of a teen-ager. The tanned freckled Elsie Pollock with perfectly tinted strawberry-blond hair exercises several times a week in a semiprivate lesson. She and her friend sit after they've showered, she says, "and have our Jarlsberg cheese and apple, and we walk out of there feeling like a million dollars. It's amazing!"

She forgets her health-food credo for her famous Texas hotdog and chili dinners. *Los Angeles* magazine's recent article on chili-makers quoted her: "One important point. I serve my beans separately. Many buffs like their chili straight. Of course I serve chopped onions and shredded Cheddar." The periodical also quoted Frank Pollock: "It's the only thing she can cook. And I don't eat it." *Los Angeles* reports her husband laughed at his clever remark. Robert Pollock, when asked if Elsie could cook, stated flatly, "No."

There is no need. She loves being a perfect hostess, and her creativity is expressed in flower-arranging. With Steuben animals. And daisies and sweet peas, for dramatic result.

Elsie Pollock loves dramatic situations. The perfect example of her ability to create spectacular yet precisely organized events occurred on Frank's seventieth birthday, another story Elsie, her husband, and their son and daughter—and Dallas employees—all love to tell. Elsie's version: "We were seated [in the pool area]. We always give gifts in the morning, and Mama and Joe [Mrs.

Frankfurt's second husband; she married again at eighty-two]
were here for breakfast. I gave Frank a few little things and one of
those little Japanese Rolls-Royce radios—we always give little
gifts—and so he turned to me and said, 'Why don't you ever give
me the real thing?' I said, 'You know I don't like big things; I like
little things.' (I'd made arrangements for them to deliver a
Rolls-Royce. . . . I'd taken Wendell [a servant] and outfitted him
in a chauffeur's uniform in case we wanted him to drive us—
Frank had always had a chauffeur in New York when we had a
limousine. I had told the man I wanted a Rolls-Royce delivered
with a *great big* red ribbon on it with two streamers.) The door-
bell rang, so Frank says, 'I wonder what that is?' and answered the door. Wendell was standing there with his new cap
on, and said, 'Mr. Pollock, your new car.' Well, I'll never forget
that as long as I live! He was *so* excited." Frank Pollock was
spotted later in the day driving along Sunset Boulevard in a
brilliant white Rolls with a red ribbon on the hood and two
streamers blowing along the sides. His wife adds: "And I got two
gold keys at Tiffany's, one for me and one for him. But he
wouldn't let me touch it! But now he'll let me drive it, but I don't
want to. No way." Penny Pollock says she thinks "Elsie is the
worst driver. She doesn't have her mind on driving. She smacks
up her Mercedes every week."

Choosing gifts for Frank gives Elsie pleasure. "It really does."
Once she bought a Steuben polar bear, an exquisite work of art,
and thought he would either love it or throw it at her, she says,
"because it sort of looks like him. He is like a bear, you know.
He'll either hug you to death or kill ya." It's all hugs for Elsie. "I
gave him a prince frog with a little gold crown"—another Steuben
beauty—because, she says, all the other frogs she kissed stayed
frogs, but Frank turned into a prince. Throaty laughter. On a
table stands a Steuben angel to remind Pollock, according to his

wife, that he married one, "in case he forgets."

And frog figures abound in the patio and pool area, visible when one is seated in the living room looking at the grounds as the interior and outdoor atmospheres blend through the glass sliding-door walls. Inside, below a painted tropical mural which covers several walls, is a long yellow sofa with two sets of flowered chairs facing one another. Chandeliers, huge plants. Pinks,

Los Angeles Times

Frank and Elsie Pollock in the living room of their Hombly Hills estate greens, coral, yellow. On the coffee table sits a sterling tray inscribed: "Never forget I love you. Elsie. 1973," presented after seven years of marriage. The plush yellow-and-white shag rug, the needlepoint pictures throughout the house—Elsie did a rendering of their Westchester County estate which hangs today in the subtropical setting—give a sunny posh feeling that starts at the lily pond near the entrance. Mrs. Pollock lives like a millionairess: "Every morning when I wake up, I can't believe it." She grew up in Dallas, Texas, but Elsie Pollock is today's California person. . . .

In Texas, Edna Ravkind sits with William Lackey, her general manager, an impeccably dressed, Dallas-bred, extraordinarily handsome man in his forties. The two met fifteen years ago; Lackey was a ballroom dance instructor and Mrs. Ravkind is an award-winning American-style and international-style dancer, remarkable for a woman in her sixties. She also executes theatre arts where partners dip, and perform lifts, and other showy maneuvers. Another Page Boy employee, whom Edna also met through her hobby, continues to do her choreography. Ballroom-dancing is the only form of relaxation Ravkind indulges in. Yet it is hardly restful. It's work.

At Page Boy, where the pursuits of work, personal affairs, social situations, decorating the Ravkind apartment, and the grooming of Edna Ravkind overlap, Lackey is often the boss's personal escort service, confidant, and protector, as well as right-hand man in the office.

Edna Ravkind exemplifies the thesis that all people would like to be eccentric—do whatever they wish, no matter how crazy—but only the rich can get away with it. "She attracts attention, deliberately," comments Lackey, who often follows behind Edna, smoothing out problems. As a waiter passes in an expensive res taurant, she'll be attracted to something on the tray and will take it. And start eating it. Another time, putting her foot up on a table, she'll turn to Lackey and ask him to adjust her shoe buckle. In elegant clothing stores she'll insist Lackey go into the fitting room with her or else she'll come out half naked, saying, "Bill, come and help me." Other examples: Mrs. Ravkind decided to cover a dress with black sequins and tiny beads, an incredibly tedious job. Visiting at Elsie's home with Lackey, she managed to spill her beads and sequins in the deep shag rug of the living room. "Hurry, Bill, before Elsie sees them!" she said, imploring him to retrieve them. So later, when she wished to pursue her sewing project during the flight home, he refused. "She knows I can only tolerate so much of this type of thing," he says. She persisted. "Please, Bill, I won't even take the beads out of the bag. I'll reach into the bag," urged Edna, in her most convincing high-pitched tones, according to Lackey. "I promise I'll not make a scene," purred Edna, suddenly a demure gray-haired slip of a woman. "Please can I sew a little? Just a little?"

Lackey relented. He remembers: "The bag falls between the seats and the beads go rolling all over the aisle. In the plane. All these little beads." Edna, in a small voice: "Oh, I'm so sorry, Bill." Adds Lackey, smiling, "That's one time I didn't pick them up." The affection for his boss shows in his face as laugh lines form around his eyes.

When she is traveling, Edna Ravkind acts as if she's at home, nonchalantly culturing milk in a motel bathroom, pulling her little plastic bag of bran from her pocketbook at a posh restaurant. Comments an employee dryly: "A very interesting person to travel with." For business and personal trips, she brings her traveling gear to work and Bill or Marge Rubin—"I work with Bill"—pack for her. "Or we go to her home and get it. . . ." The three discuss what she's taking for several days before the trip. Rubin comments, "If the packing's not done before she leaves, she goes ahead and then we get it together and send it, or take it to her and come back."

Traveling and at work, Ravkind expresses her individuality. Once she entered Page Boy's executive offices, with its adjoining retail shop, only a few days after a face-lift. The suture threads were dangling around her eyes; she was bruised-looking. This, however, did not deter her from waiting on a customer, who just stared. When she had a chance, the pregnant buyer asked, "What happened to her?" assuming Ravkind was injured in a terrible accident.

Edna Ravkind is a dichotomy. She takes great pains to create an elegant fall wardrobe—she's a size six or eight—and yet, comments an employee, on another day she will come to work with a scarf around her head, "looking like hell," remove it, and her hair will be standing on end, for she coated it in olive oil the previous night and is letting it soak in. Once someone suggested she cake her hair with Vaseline and she did, "and showed up at the office that way." Perhaps she enjoys shocking others. "She'll get up and wait on customers looking like that. And of course the customer is in such awe." The employee goes on, "It kills me. I don't understand it. She'll conduct business with visitors from New York and dry her hair at the same time. In rollers. She'll ask them to speak louder because she cannot hear them over the dryer."

But she can be incredibly vain—to the point where she had plastic surgery. And cold and calculating. Associates say she is a phony when she is using you, yet "is straight about letting you know one way or another if she does not care for you." (The three sisters share these traits, acquaintances feel.)

William Lackey attributes much of the eccentricity to his boss's femininity and would not take it from a male boss. He says Edna Ravkind is a mother-image to him. "Yes. Very definitely."

Edna Ravkind flanked by associates Marge Rubin and Bill Lackey

She is mother to three children: Billy, a Dallas criminal lawyer; Sidney, a union attorney; and Joan (Mrs. Ari) Sussman, a jet-setter, yet down to earth and totally different from her mother, according to a friend. An acquaintance says Edna's family role was more like the traditional paternal place—and she was "a lousy father"—while her husband, Abe, acting as Mother, stayed home raising the children. Emotionally, Edna is closer to Page Boy (Bill Lackey and Marge Rubin included), employees claim she has commented.

Today she lives in her expensive condominium in downtown Dallas with Abe. Like her offices, the home has sliding mirrored surfaces, is elegantly decorated, but Ravkind enjoys retiring in a sleeping bag on her living-room floor with a hot-water bag and a mini-TV. And she offers no explanation.

Eccentric. Employees admit to discussing Edna—and Elsie—at cocktail parties. Comments and observations by employees and acquaintances: "A hard worker to the point of exhaustion." "She changes her mind from moment to moment." "A more human person than Mrs. Pollock." "She loves to say, 'I've changed my mind'. . . sometimes to show she has that power." "Can look great or 'the pits.'" "Explosions!" "Without her dancing she's a very lonely person." "She continues to mesmerize me. What is she going to do next?" "Really a warm person toward people she likes." "She has 'developed' taste." "She throws out ideas and wants you to choose the best of them. You have to first categorize the different things." "She plays dumb to get something from some-one." "She will not even complete a sentence before she's begun another. And another. And another." "I know exactly what she's saying although no one else does [Lackey's comment]." "They don't pay well." "Unprofessional." "When forced into a corner, she'll make a decision." "She's a crusty, hard person to get to know." "Smart!"

... Elsie Pollock walks past the indoor aviary toward her kitchen as light filters through one of the many skylights of the house. Frank Pollock has just arrived with fresh meat from a farmer's market, and shows his purchases to Elsie, who, carrying the bundles to her scale, studies the weight readings and announces her magnate husband has been cheated.

The purchases are logged in a record book indicating weight (Elsie's, not the butcher's), price, cut, and date. As the kitchen help eventually prepare these various meats for a meal, they add that date, and the ultimate use of the food. Elsie runs her home as one would manage a business. ...

Throughout her business career, Mrs. Pollock has been considered to be frugal by her associates. Edna on Elsie: "To the penny. To the last little dumb. ... She can't stand to mark down a dress. If you left it to Elsie, you would never mark down a dress." Bill Lackey says Elsie Pollock spends hours going over figures and analyzing them and then re-analyzing them. And Penny Pollock di Grazia states, "Elsie never spends money. I mean never. It's that frugal kind of non-waste Jewish ethnic thing," and says the Rolls-Royce gift was "the shock of the century."

Elsie is the finance person; Edna Ravkind will not look at a figure, according to Frank Pollock, who says the older sister does not know "if she's got two or ten million." Edna compares her sister to an actress: "There'll never be enough fame or money . . ." She leaves the sentence unfinished. A moment later she adds, with a smile, "And I was always glad I got half the money."

But not half the fame. Elsie received it all: advisory board of the graduate business school at the University of Southern California, Southern Methodist University's Woman of the Year,

"Dinah!" TV-show guest, a *Mademoiselle* magazine outstanding woman, model for Camel cigarettes ad (although she does not smoke), first woman elected to the Young President's Organization (and, as she passed the cutoff age of forty-nine, one of the 10 percent of Y.P.O. members elevated to the chief executive board), written up in *Life, Fortune,* and sent by the United States government to Tunisia to evaluate America's role in helping the undeveloped country ("They needed a token. I was it").

In Texas, Edna Ravkind says she has never been recognized for her contributions to Page Boy. Associates notice that when the sisters are together Mrs. Ravkind always takes the back seat, because "that's been the pattern all these years."

A fragile peacock of a woman, Edna considers her sisterly relationship with her closed-lip smile, stands and walks past a hanging mirror ball toward the stairwell.

The second floor of the Dallas headquarters of Page Boy contains a working area with cutting tables, sewing machines, samples, and patterns. All manufacturing used to be done here but today only designs and sample dresses are produced on location. Much of the clothing sporting the Page Boy label is made by others, and Page Boy's two hundred employees are mainly involved in sales; about fifteen are in the manufacturing and design division.

Downstairs again, Mrs. Ravkind sits behind her desk—with Bill Lackey on one side, Marge Rubin on the other—and comments that if the maternity-wear business was easy, "everyone would be in it. . . . They come and they go."

The telephone rings. Elsie Pollock is calling from California; excepting the California operation, she is involved with the business by phone mainly—"when it doesn't conflict with her social activities," says an employee. Marge Rubin—a twenty-two-year employee—says, "Mrs. Ravkind is truly the backbone of the company. She's the one who's here day in and day out."

Page Boy Maternity Fashions has through the years wholesaled its fashions to Saks, Jordan Marsh, Garfinckel's, Bonwit's, Lord & Taylor, Henri Bendel's, Catherine's in Hawaii, Bergdorf's, Marshall Field, Neiman-Marcus. Past and present customers include Alice Faye, Margaret Sullavan, Jayne Meadows, Barbra Streisand, Ali MacGraw, Florence Henderson, Errol Flynn's wife ("She was impossible," says Edna), Mrs. Lamar Hunt, all the Neiman-Marcus women. When asked if a pregnant woman could look sexy, Bill Lackey says, "Definitely." Marge Rubin comments, "Oh, yes." Edna, after hesitation, pipes, "Maybe . . ."

This past year has been the best in Page Boy's history. A good day in their own shops is around three to four thousand dollars retail, with four employees. Although Edna Ravkind makes decisions concerning stores she oversees while Elsie Pollock is in charge of her California shops—a significant portion of the total business—corporate decisions are reached jointly. Bill Lackey believes that independently the sisters would not have been as successful as they have been, "because they each worked in different areas, and together they were able to make it a whole." But, he adds, two charmers would have been impossible, so Edna held back. He remembers, "When I met Elsie, I was fascinated not only by her beauty but by her charm and her mind. I fell in love with her. It was a fantasy. . . . To appreciate her intelligence and recognize her drive presents a challenge to be able to work with someone like that. I have great respect for her."

Two sisters, each with complementing talents. Edna Ravkind—birdlike, youthful for her seventy years, eccentric—

handles a large share of the daily workload, while Pollock—chic, glamorous—is the visible public-relations sister.

Elsie has her practical business side as well. In addition to being a monetary watchdog, she is an expert seamstress (remember, she made that first dress) who has worn some designer clothes forever, often taking them apart at the seams and creating totally new outfits. Employees tell of the double-faced woollen Givenchy coat Elsie remade by removing the interior, relining the garment, and making a skirt from the old lining. "And it looked absolutely magnificent." One of her employees was overheard telling a customer, "Our head alteration lady, Mrs. Pollock, will do that for you while you wait," and Elsie has been seen in the back room ripping a hem and putting in a new one for a customer. Often she'll take alterations home.

And there is Edna's eye for fashion, which appears instinctive but co-workers insist she developed. Ravkind regularly chooses what eventually will be the profitable maternity attire.

Complementing each other's abilities while sharing a business in a difficult industry, the Frankfurt sisters have made it work even when relations were strained—although Edna claims her sister has marvelous control, does not lose her temper. She suggests Bill Lackey will verify this. Lackey: "Her voice rises." Perhaps an understatement.

"They scream and yell," states another employee, out of Edna's earshot. Years ago, Elsie was doing an out-of-town trunk show, where designers show their fashions, when she called her sister in Dallas insisting she needed additional merchandise immediately. A worker relates: "That created a real thorn in Mrs. Ravkind's side. So she went up to the shipping room. . . ." Orders were being filled for Saks Fifth Avenue, Lord & Taylor, stores throughout the United States—thousands of garments. Edna ordered them all shipped to Elsie instead, that afternoon. "There was not one hanger hanging." According to employees, the mess was never straightened out. "Everyone was packing, no records were made, nothing." Nobody seems to know how the original demand and Edna's reaction to it were resolved between the sisters.

Edna leans back in the booth of an expensive downtown Dallas restaurant and wipes her petite mouth daintily. One can imagine her ears perking up as she converses.

Question: It's worked out well for the two of you, hasn't it?

Ravkind, dryly: "Well, we made money."

6

MEDICAL MOUSETRAP

Janet M. Esty

JANET MARIE DEARHOLT ESTY is founder and president of the
Boulder-based medical-electronics firm, Neomed. Neomed
manufactures, among other items, an electronic surgical instrument, Neoknife, a modernized version of the scalpel. Before the
development of this type of cutting tool, the scalpel used in the
operating room cut like a kitchen knife. Today physicians "burn"
with the electronic instrument, using a highly directional spark at
the end of the knife, rather than slicing through tissue. This
simultaneously cauterizes potential bleeding areas. Neoknife has
an added electronic coagulating feature, causing blood to clot.

Entering the Neomed offices, one sees a notice on the door
that reads: "ASSEMBLERS WANTED, APPLY WITHIN." A giant
Neoknife—a mock-up of the electronic scalpel-coagulator—
stands in a corner of the reception area. When its buttons are
pressed, it emits one sound for cutting and another for coagulating. *Forbes* magazines sit on the coffee table and another sign
indicates: "ATTENTION: ESCORT REQUIRED BEYOND THIS POINT."

127

Neoknife's instruction sheet hangs on the wall, in Italian, Japanese, French, Spanish, Finnish, and an African dialect.

Upstairs a long hallway ends at Esty's office. Behind her desk is a poster, "Top of the World," depicting the Rocky Mountains; old medical books and an antique electronics volume are open behind her desk. A Christmas plant, still with its dusty red tin foil, sits on one of the shelves near *Business Monthly, Duties and Liabilities of Corporation Officers,* and *Directors and Corporate Planning.*

Janet Esty, president, is at her desk. In her late thirties, Esty initially comes across tough. Within five minutes she relates how she told an irritating business associate to "fuck off." The tenacity and hardness perhaps began to develop as she was growing up in the small town of Bemidji, in cold northern Minnesota, a hundred miles from the Canadian border. The second child in a family of five—four girls and a boy—her home life was, according to her, "reasonably supportive. From the time I was big enough to carry anything, I did my share." A vacant lot next to the house was farmed, Esty remembers, and, she says, "Even when we were little kids, every spring we took our little red wagons and peddled our vegetables all over town. We all had paper routes; I think we all learned basic mathematics that way."

The Dearholt family ancestors came to Minnesota from Germany as homesteaders in the early 1900s. When Janet was in elementary school, her parents—financially strapped—decided to move to the homesteaded land they still owned, and Esty remembers getting up at six o'clock to study flute, then schoolwork, before milking cows.

Nedra Dearholt, Janet's mother, left school and married at sixteen. As her husband turned to farming after being a mechanic for years, she decided to open a music store in Bemidji. Before the retail business, she worked as a seamstress in a Munsingwear factory. "So she really started this store, and after two or three years my dad came in on it, too," Janet remembers. The shop began to thrive.

Janet's father, a graduate of a two-year business school, was a practical, intelligent man, expert at home repairs and projects. Nedra Dearholt, who separated from her husband in 1976, says, "In my private life with me he was gentle. He found it difficult to show affection to the children." Her daughter Janet says she feels "Father is a very cold person," while she sees her mother as a warm and shining success who developed her music business to the point where other companies were vying to buy it. A helpful individual, verbally loving toward her children rather than physically so, Nedra Dearholt comments on the family: "We used to say there were too many chiefs and not enough Indians.... *Everybody* was a strong person. Every one of them is an achiever."

Coming from a musically oriented family, Janet taught piano in the store for six to eight hours daily. As a teen-ager, she realized her decision to be both a concert pianist and a surgeon was unrealistic; she chose medicine.

While she was an excellent secondary student, there was pressure for her to do better. No matter what his children did, Mr. Dearholt did not consider it enough. The unpleasant home situation affected Janet's two older sisters and brother; all left home before their high school graduation. (And Janet soon followed.)

In high school Janet was interested in older boys. She quips, "I suppose my mom understood and my dad understood too well." Mrs. Dearholt says, "Janet dated earlier than I would have approved." She started spending time with boys while she was in junior high school. When asked if she was in love with someone during her high-school years, she answered, with a smile, "Several." A physically early maturer, she was not the "frilly popular type," yet males were interested in her. At that time, she considered marriage unnecessary and could not fathom the reason for it—perhaps because of her parents' difficulties. "It was a very unhappy household. . . . Very high-pressure environment at home," she recalls. The problems with her violent father (Question: Did he knock you around? Answer: "Yep.") increased to the point where she rented an apartment with a girl friend.

She eloped on senior skip day in 1960.

Her marriage took place at an Army Reserve camp where her husband, Jerry Esty, was spending the weekend. (Question: Were you pregnant? Answer: "I won't answer that question." Laughter.) After the wedding, Jerry, an unskilled high-school graduate, worked at a local gas station. She finished high school, and they moved to Nebraska.

While waiting for the child's birth, she taught piano. She remembers being in labor for three days and "pretty sore after. But," she says, "I couldn't wait until the baby came and I could get out of that house. I was going just absolutely bananas." She adds that the newborn, Andrea, was a "beautiful little thing . . . absolutely marvelous," yet, "I was so glad I could find baby-sitters that were good to her, to leave her with. . . . All the time I was in the hospital I knitted and knitted. Oh, my God, I tried *so* hard to get some motherly instinct going." Unsuccessfully. Janet, a seventeen-year-old mother, felt little for the child. An honest, forthright woman, she realizes she had some maturing to do.

The new mother heard of a job in Omaha, at a soup company plucking chickens, and was chagrined to find they wouldn't hire her until her seven-day-old child was six weeks. So she went to a local employment agency.

Although she had never studied typing in high school, her parents gave her a typewriter, upon graduation, with a self-teach record. The employment agency explained typing was necessary for most positions, and required she take a test. Her speed was twelve words a minute, "with about eighty-five errors." Esty went home and practiced. When she went to the agency the next day, the interviewer asked why she wished to repeat the test so soon. She explained, "Today I know how to type." Once again she did poorly, went home, and practiced. Assuming her piano expertise would help, she says, "I worked all day long on that damn typing record."

On the third day, she went for her typing test: "Everybody laughed a lot. Called everybody over." (Esty frequently omits the first word of a sentence.) A great believer in feedback, she asked after the test where she was and the level of typing expertise required. It was necessary to type thirty-five words a minute to qualify for a clerical position.

The fourth day, she recalls, "They put me in this room, with all the people peeking through the door, and I thought, I'll show you. . . . Thirty-five words per minute, with something like thirty-five errors! Then an old man—this great big honker—received a telephone call. The missile base was just organizing and needed a receptionist who could handle people and problems, who was tough. Union guys would be coming through and they needed someone for the hiring office. Honker said, 'I think we have the person for you.'"

At the base she listened to words she had never heard before: "Expanded my vocabularity 4,000 percent. Unbelievable . . . I think I had lived a fairly sheltered life." The men worked on oil rigs, and, she says, "The last time I ever blushed was in that office."

After work, she went home to a kind, sensitive spouse. "He thought I was violent." Her laughter erupts. The Estys both worked seven days a week: "Stashed away lots of bucks. Left the kid with a baby-sitter." But Jerry—who, Janet says, was content—recognized his young wife was not happy; he knew the intelligent teen-ager, who had been awarded and had to refuse three scholarships, wanted a college education. Now she was not pregnant and could attend school, but scholarships were no longer forthcoming.

They moved back to Minnesota, where they had residency and a tuition reduction, and both planned to attend college. Jerry Esty had no desire for education; Janet "pep-talked" him into it.

In Bemidji they bought a tiny home with their savings, and Janet Esty told her husband she wished a divorce.

"My husband was a very good person who was in no way matched to me. . . . What I knew was I didn't in any way want this marriage." She had no feelings for him, although, she says, "He cared about the baby and was very good to both of us." Did she suddenly realize this as she began to attend college? Was there some connection? "No, it hit me from the day I got married." Janet Esty's mother talks of the marriage: "As a person I liked Jerry. But it was so pitiful—that's the only word I can use—because there were never two people who were so mismatched. They had absolutely *nothing* in common."

Without arguing, they split everything. Except the house and the baby. Esty says, deadpan, in her husky voice: "I lucked out. I got the kid. . . . [Laughter. Then a serious voice.] I really feel if a young woman decides the marriage is not working and the husband is more mature and he really wants the child, then the woman should give the kid to the father." At the time of her divorce, "it was not the thing to do," but she realizes today that Jerry Esty was in a better frame of mind to care for Andrea, and "society would have been kinder to him."

Although the court ordered child-support, Janet Esty would not accept it: "This was going to be a clean break." She told him, "You forget about the kid. Forget about paying for her—I'll pay

for her—and stay off my back." Though he was unhappy about
the arrangement, her husband had no choice. Looking back, she
sees this as a horrible thing to have done to Jerry, who remarried
and now lives in Minnesota with a young son. A college
graduate, he teaches high-school industrial arts. About five years
ago, Janet Esty did some soul-searching and arranged for her
ex-husband and daughter to become acquainted.

The divorced mother soon was confronted with her daughter
being sent home by the parents of neighborhood playmates because Andrea was from a broken family. Esty says the attitude was
"We don't expect a divorced person to take good care of her
children." And she remembers P.T.A. meetings scheduled in the
daytime which were impossible for her to attend. She juggled
jobs around, however, and managed. As a result of these experiences, she is not a women's libber. She says, "These matrons
who now are going through their change of life, who suddenly
decide they are going to divorce and expect the world to be good
to them and want the world to help them get their lives together— Sorry, I won't forget the shit they handed out fifteen
years ago. . . . 'Hey, baby, think back what you did. I never would
have done to your kid what you did to mine.'" Esty agrees she is
somewhat vindictive: "Because they hurt my kid." The sense of
protectiveness for her only child is strong. Often her reactions
and choice of words—referring to her child as "the kid"—suggest
an insensitivity. With time and familiarity, her warmth becomes
apparent. And her decisiveness.

Esty was determined to obtain a college education on her own.
She did not turn to her parents. "I didn't want their help, and in
particular I didn't want anything to do with my father." Figuring
"to the penny" the amount necessary to earn in addition to her
savings—with calculations for baby-sitting costs and living
expenses—she decided two and a half years of schooling could be

managed financially. She says she planned to "cram four years of education into that time period. And I did it. Taught music lessons to forty students. Worked a lot. Never saw my kid. I was fortunate in that I found a super lady, who had raised her own family, who loved Andrea. I dropped her off in the morning and she would be sleeping, and I would pick her up at night and she would be sleeping."

During these years, Esty drank heavily and "lived hard." She believed in marriage even less then than she had in high school: "Preachers on the one end and lawyers on the other; these are the only ones who make out in marriage."

"I finished college and planned to go to medical school." In her family there was no such word as "can't." Employees today say it drives them crazy when she constantly chides them, "There's no such word as can't."

"Totally flat broke." Her monetary education plan worked out "right to the button." Nothing was left. Moving into what she calls "slumsville" with her young daughter in a run-down area of Minneapolis, she lived in a "big old barn of a house, with fireplaces and charm, at sixty dollars a month." Streetwalkers passed the house at night. "Didn't need a TV." An Indian family lived in their car in the back yard and there were "powwows in the front yard every Saturday night. . . . Every time Andrea went outside to play, an old man came to her with a winebottle in one hand and handed her a nickel with the other." They had fun living there, she cheerfully says, and laughs. An optimist, nothing seems to knock Esty down. Perhaps these challenges all added fuel to her fire.

With her college degree, she obtained a position in a University of Minnesota biochemistry laboratory. "Took a job as a junior scientist at four hundred and sixty-eight dollars a month." Almost fifteen years later, she remembers salaries to the dollar.

Although it was less than she had earned at the missile base, Esty enjoyed the work—cancer research—and hoped the university position would expedite her entrance to medical school.

While she was a biochemist dreaming of surgery, she became irritated with the neighborhood's demonstrating welfare mothers: "I was the only person within a six-block radius who went to work, but I couldn't find a baby-sitter. I found it fascinating that all these people had time to march. . . . That's when I started to get angry." After getting an education while also supporting herself and Andrea, it was, she says, infuriating to be also bankrolling welfare mothers who refused to baby-sit for pay, yet demanded free college educations for their children.

Esty continued to pursue surgical-education possibilities, and when she was offered a teaching assistantship in the sciences at $250 a month at the University of Minnesota (which included attending their graduate school), she decided to accept. "Wasn't hot on the idea," but she felt graduate credits might facilitate her entrance to medical school. Planning to teach piano to supplement the small salary, she found her lab course required twenty-four hours a week at the school. She says, "It was going to cost me eighty dollars for a baby-sitter for that one course." She spoke to her graduate adviser about the problem. "We had a lack of meeting of the minds. . . . I quit grad school after one month."

By this time, Esty recognized she could never attend medical school. "I'd never be able to afford it. . . . I was a little pissed as I looked around and saw all the people getting government aid, and if you tried to do it yourself. . . ." Medical school would have been possible had she accepted welfare, she believes. "They would have paid for it then." Did you consider that? "No. Would you?" Self-reliant, abrupt, she says, "I'd walk the streets before I'd go on welfare."

After her short stint as a graduate student, she found a position in industry—"where you can make more money"—at $600 a month. As a technical writer for Univac Corporation, she headed her department within four years and "built a new thing called data management, which was taking care of all the paper work and reporting requirements for government contracts.

"Got a bellyful of that."

As she tells the story of her life, in her husky voice, Esty does not exude the kind of natural self-confidence bred into many, but a tougher ego hacked out of granite. Often she keeps her eyes upward as she reminisces, and then suddenly those serious, staring eyes fall upon the listener with a startling directness.

Esty moved from the lovely home in the run-down neighborhood while working at Univac. She says, "I found a great big old house for sale in the university district," and she decided that if she boarded four college students in the four bedrooms and decorated the basement to rent a couple of more rooms, she'd collect rent from six individuals and she and Andrea could live "in the dining room and the kitchen and whatever." Esty says she found a banker "who believed in me. I explained my game plan." She provided for-rent ads showing rates and brought backup material indicating she had researched the project. He was impressed: "He is one of the people who I think deserves some points, because that was before it was popular [to accept a divorced woman as a mortgagee]." She bought the house and became a landlord.

At her newest job, a man with a position parallel to hers but with half the number of people reporting to him was making 40 percent more than she. In addition, her job "took more moxie." Esty—never one to be taken advantage of—complained, received little satisfaction, and, she says, "I told my boss to stuff his lousy job."

At about this time, a Minneapolis firm called Medtronics had designed and built one of the original cardiac pacemakers, and she remembers thinking, Gee, that sounds neat. That's medical, electronics, innovative. Space age. All kinds of neat things. She applied for a position with the company. There were no openings, and the relentless Esty regularly checked back until she was hired as a medical writer, creating instruction manuals for physicians and training materials for salesmen, and working in the marketing department. This company, which she refers to as "the granddaddy of medical electronics," was an exciting place. Many who were originally employed there left to start their own companies; this one corporation has spawned perhaps a hundred small businesses.

After about eighteen months—in 1967 and 1968—Esty decided to find a small blooming company where she could get in "on the ground floor" and make a greater impression.

The company she found was in Boulder, Colorado, and she started there as a technical writer when Andrea was eight. Since her daughter's birth, she had no time to herself, no vacations. There were heavy involvements with men, some serious, but Esty says today: "I'm a great believer in coming and going. You live fast. . . . I've always said that it was a damn good thing that I had my daughter. Because I was raised to be very responsible about parenthood." She thinks this kept her from joining the Weathermen—and laughs heartily at her semi-joke—or becoming involved with drugs. "I think it's constantly fine-tuning when you first start out on your own. You're swinging this way and that way. And as you get further along you say, 'Well, this is not very productive and that was pretty self-destructive.'"

Esty rented a house near her new job, in a residential-industrial area of the small, suntanned college town of Boulder, with a view of the foothills of the Rockies. "I *really* thought I had what I was looking for. And I worked my rear end off." But the company was not stable. "Guy number two bounced guy number

one out of his own company." The situation cast a pall; she
started looking for another job.

The rumor she might be job-hunting reached her boss, who
asked, "Are you staying or are you going?" Her natural reaction
when she is put in a corner is to say goodbye. She did.

Although, as she says, "I really didn't have my act together,
hadn't decided what I was going to do," Esty knew she enjoyed
the medical field of electrosurgery. With two men who also quit,
she decided to launch a company. One of the men had an engineering background, the other was knowledgeable about manufacturing, and she knew marketing.

"So we started Neomed in March of 1971. Struggled along.
Starving to death." They rented a dim room above a paint store.
"Go down a dark hallway and you'll find it." Esty became president. "One of them suggested it, the other seconded it, and I
didn't disagree." Laughter. She was people-oriented and they
weren't. "None of us were competent. I was the least incompe-
tent." One was ten years older, and the other a couple of years
younger, than she.

By December, one partner was "getting a lot of heat from his
wife, who didn't like starving to death" and was irritated that she
might "occasionally have to go to work to make things work," so
her husband left the company. The other partner left shortly
thereafter. ("I've had him back here a couple of times when he
was in a financial pinch.") "So all of a sudden I was left with the
company," two years after its inception.

While the firm was struggling, she approached friends for capital for the manufacture of prototypes and "raised fifty thousand
bucks . . . in five-thousand-dollar increments." Before her
partners left, they built the first Neoknife models themselves, a
product produced by their ex-employer but, they believed, improved upon. Esty rented what equipment was needed, bought

soldering irons, and procured samples of parts where possible. "Beg, borrow, and steal anything you can get yours hands on. That's when you figure out how to cut all the corners. That's when you live or die." Cash had to be spent on certain trappings such as the printing of letterheads, but Esty used motel stationery when she could—and, when she was traveling, brought Andrea hotel soap bars as gifts. Esty says her partners—and most men— will "go out and buy a desk calendar when from my standpoint you stop at a gas station and ask if they have any free calendars." She is irritated that her present-day employees have the same mandarin attitude. "You don't see the average guy in business thinking in terms of how to cut corners." She purchased no pencils, staples, or pads at the beginning. "I find it interesting how a guy can't operate unless he has a store-bought file." And does she take packaged sugar from restaurant sugar bowls? "No, that is going too far." Esty does differentiate between a visible business with an image to maintain and one never visited by customers. Her own flavorless office contains piled concrete blocks forming bookshelves. Esty points out that people do not come to her to see the product. National salesmen visit the customer.

During the six months it took to get the first product on the market, Esty "bought nothing" and lived on the money realized from the sale of her Minneapolis boarding house. The banker had been right; she lived there for five years rent-free and made fourteen thousand dollars when it was sold.

Neomed's first order—from a distributor—was for two hundred generators, the power plant for an electronic scalpel, selling for $2,500 in direct competition with a product manufactured by her previous employer. (To this date, she has sold over two thousand of these generators, one of Neomed's forty items.)

With over twenty-five representatives in this country and about

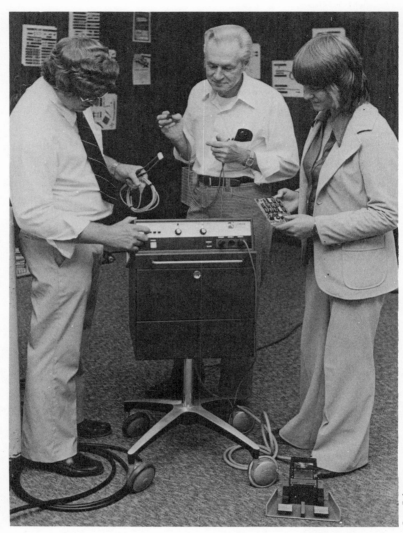

President and sole officer, Janet Esty, and employees, with Neoknife's generator. To the left is a competitor's earlier unit

thirty outside the United States, and selling to such major medical institutions as Scripps in La Jolla, the Massachusetts General Hospital, St. Luke's in Houston, the Hospital of Special Surgery in New York, Temple Medical College of Pennsylvania, St. Mary's in Rochester, and Stanford, Esty considers diversifying, with her emphasis continuing in medicine. On her entrepreneurial experiences: "To me work is not a dirty word. I really love what I am doing and always have. I figure if you work hard and you're smart, you can make money. . . . If you're going to do the right things, you will get the money automatically."

Neomed Corporation is in an industrialized section of Boulder, with a mountain view from its offices and work areas. In her second-floor office, Esty leans back in her chair next to a hanging Arabian rug—the one decorating touch. A lover of sayings, she has a wallful in her office and throughout the Neomed Building:

> **Does it increase profit? Increase sales?**
> **Decrease costs? Improve communication?**

With smoke spiraling from her constantly lit but usually not smoked cigarette and with a half-full coffee mug on her desk, Esty talks about being the boss: "Your problems are not things, your problems are people. Must take care of them. Be concerned and hope it will be reciprocal. Hard finding the right people in terms of doing the work."

Today Neomed has about fifty employees. One, the sales manager, Don Battles—slow-speaking, with that distinctive classy pizzazz some black men possess—is a personal friend of Esty's. A University of Minnesota graduate, Don met Esty at Medtronics about a decade ago. His first comment about his boss:

"I respect her." Battles explains the reason for Neomed's success: "Janet built a better mousetrap."

The man with the new idea is a crank until the idea succeeds.

Battles insists Neomed's products work better than their competitor's in the solid-state electrosurgery industry, which started and continues to be centered in Boulder. The well-dressed, totally bald sales manager sits in an unpretentious office, with a map of United States hospitals behind his desk, and describes Esty as "an honest honorable person whose word means something in the classical sense." Battles acknowledges no differences between having a male boss or Esty. "I don't. I think a lot of men would. But that's their problem." He says Esty is willing to "back off" if it's practical, even if she's convinced she's right. "That's one of the reasons for her success." Esty is, according to him, a logical person who knows her own worth but is sometimes impatient and forgets to take other people's feelings into consideration: "The unique thing about Janet is that she is totally committed. She sacrifices a lot. She *has* to sacrifice a lot. . . . She ought to take a vacation once in a while."

Esty's teen-age daughter, who has worked for Neomed as an assembler, agrees. Her mother talks about the possibility of their vacationing, yet she is constantly working. Esty, when asked what she does during a typical weekend if she's not working, answers, "I'm working." Her life today includes a house in the country. She does not ski. "No time." What do you like to spend money on? "Nothing." Clothes? "No." With light green eyes, the five-foot-six-inch woman has a pale pallor in comparison with the tanned young residents of this bathed-in-sunshine town. (Boulder, Colorado, must have more joggers per mile than any other city in the country.) Not a swimmer, she says, "I really don't do anything. I don't think I relax much." Her cigarette continues to burn in its ashtray and a long ash grows. She rubs her chin in a masculine way.

A solid businesswoman, she spends her time in her office behind her desk, near bookcases holding *Gray's Anatomy, The Way Things Work,* a book titled *Up Your Own Business Organization* ("a morale-lifter, nutsy-boltsy advice"). She doesn't read *Harvard Business Review:* "That's a pain in the ass." Papers are neatly piled on her desk. "I'm well organized to a fault." And she adds that she does not believe anyone can be too organized.

> **Genius is superlative attention to minute details.**

In keeping with her love of work and organization, she also believes in hindsight. "I don't like to make the same mistake a second time. Made enough the first time around and would prefer not to repeat them." Before her laugh is heard, there is an almost silent hissing. Then the laugh waves burst forth and she sounds happy. She says she likes to analyze the good and the bad that happen, and figure out why. "Horrible lecturer," she says of herself. Employees agree.

> **Around here I have a very responsible position.**
> **Whenever something goes wrong, I'm responsible.**

She remembers when her business began: "I was going through some terrible times. And I really got tough. I *had* to get tough. . . . I quit asking and started telling. Quit taking too much lip."

> **Do something, period.**
> **Either lead, follow or get the hell out of the way.**

With short, blunt hair, cut once a year and self-trimmed in between ("when I can't see out any more"), she wears no lipstick, nail polish, makeup. "Just pure raw beauty.", Followed by hearty laughter. Characteristically, she is amused at this joke about herself. Jewelry? "No." No time for men, either, she says.

Esty stares into space when she is talking, but then her eyes focus on the listener again. Her broad face looks amused as she explains that the important thing in her life is minimum hassle. Example: she owns a "very reliable old hog," her older-model car. The engine works and she'll continue to drive it as long as it functions. However, she recognizes the business community assesses success by what one drives. Her salespeople comment often on her car. "I'm starting to listen." Sales manager Battles: "She's got a real thing about that old car of hers." Discussions with employees and her daughter indicate this conversation has gone on for years.

The logical Esty—with a rare rebellion against reason—is fanatical about keeping the hassles out of her life to the point where she refuses to buy a washer or a dryer. Her daughter says her mother buys seventy pairs of panties at a time, and Esty explains—laughing at herself good-naturedly—this is because she goes to the laundromat only once every three months. Having an appliance break down requires a serviceman. A hassle. Instead she puts fourteen laundry baskets in her station wagon and heads for the laundromat. About once every ninety days. She bursts out laughing at the ludicrous mental image. But she keeps on doing it.

During a rare social evening, Esty unwinds, laughs, and enjoys herself. She loves a joke and her cynical sense of humor is apparent. Although she can be fun-loving and silly, she is always aware of what she is saying.

> **What I want is all of the power and none of the responsibility.**

Often serious, Esty shows her softer side at Neomed through music. She is, for her own enjoyment, still a pianist, and a peppy whistler, a pro. Her birdlike changes in key, her tone and resonance exemplify her musical talent. She hums as well. Her secretary says Esty whistles constantly, "nonstop," and often does scales.

Listening to the unusual whistling, one tends to forget this persistent young woman's tough aura. Perhaps, as with many successful females, the years of self-achievement will soften the edges and allow her to forget the struggles. But today she still remembers them.

She recalls rumors which circulated during her first Neomed years that she was sleeping with the banker, the manufacturers' representatives, and other stepping stones. When this died down, "lesbianism" was whispered. "I found that it just *crushed* me." Working late with a key male employee, she was discussing a project with him over a drink when he said to her, "I'm curious. None of us knows anything about your social life. . . . Do you like women?" Her response: "I canned him." Silent laughter. Yet at the time she reacted with shock and horror, and she says, "If I were a crying-type person, then I would have cried. As it was, I think I just sat there with my mouth hanging open." Her decision to fire the employee was based upon her feeling that his impressions would be contagious. "And no way could I deal with that." She told him to find a job with "a big burly macho guy," and added, "No, I don't like women."

Make the most of your own misery. It may not last forever.

This woman, who never relaxes or takes vacations and doesn't enjoy spending her money, digs a garden every spring. "And every fall I go out and look and see who won." She calls it her one-month catharsis. The digging is important, not what is planted or grows.

Esty digs, prods, grinds. But she wonders if other women wishing to enter the business world will be able to make it. "Most have low self-images which extrapolate back to other women." She finds females more formal with a man—even though the male might have no authority—versus the "You're my sister" attitude they assume with another woman in a position of power, often automatically using first names. "It is hard to be objective about such women, because I immediately say to myself, 'Hmmm, they don't know the rules of business.'" They often lack, according to Esty, an acumen of polish, and "it turns male co-workers off when they must introduce their associate, who is this giggly, silly, ill-dressed woman; it knocks the man's ego, for he's saying essentially, 'This is my equal.'" Esty's secretary says, "I call her Jan, but in front of other people I call her Mrs. Esty." Correct, feels Esty, and relates the time she met important business visitors in the reception area, where her receptionist said: "'This is Mr. So-and-So, this is Mr. So-and-So, and this is Dr. So-and-So . . . and this is Jan.' . . . That gal destroyed me, my ability to negotiate. . . . There was a startled expression on the men's faces and . . . a more than startled expression on mine. It was pure horror." While Esty was figuring how to recoup the situation, her secretary came in and asked each man—using his title—if he would like coffee, and then finished with "Jan, how about you?" Esty had a serious talk with her employees the next day about the importance of ground rules. Afterward she was amused by undercurrent employee reactions: *"Jan* now wants to be called *Mrs. Esty."* Esty points out that men who work for her would never make this type of mistake: "Women have to stop hitting men over the head for their discriminatory practices and think about what they are doing to themselves."

Esty does not have close female friends. "Not any more. I have more in common with most men." The women she associates with are her mother, who is a Neomed purchasing agent; her

Esty holds Neomeds electric scalpel, Neoknife

The Sunday Camera

daughter; and employees such as Barbara Hardy.

Hardy, Esty's accountant for over five years, rose to this position in an unusual manner. Esty recognized her department heads were ineffectual, yet work was being done by someone. She found in each case an underling was actually doing the labor and taking on the responsibility, but not receiving credit. She fired her heads of departments and elevated the individuals who were efficient, regardless of education or experience. One of these was Barbara Hardy.

Originally hired as a clerk, this woman with a high-school education is, according to Esty, topnotch. Barbara Hardy says, "I could always snow my male bosses. . . . Women [bosses] expect more of you, and can't be snowed. And especially Jan." Her boss, a "very down-to-earth person," is a perfectionist. Although Mrs. Hardy was not hired as a typist, Esty felt she should be proficient in this skill. "She used to say, 'You can do anything you want to,'" Hardy says. Esty, with her own experience learning to type, finally accepted the fact that Hardy would never be a typist. The accountant feels her boss is "a woman who knows where she is going. . . . She stays here until the wee hours of the night and is seldom here later than eight-thirty in the morning." Energetic. And dedicated. Hardy remembers that once in five years her boss was ill. Mrs. Hardy does feel Esty has a "nit-pick thing about office supplies. That used to drive me nuts," she says. "You couldn't have more than one pencil or pen in your drawer." Esty is softening a bit in this direction, her employee feels.

Hardy does not see her boss as a particularly feminine woman; she will "come down hard" if an employee is lax, but it is obviously never a personal attack. Esty often philosophizes on the concept of team effort, according to Hardy. Temper? "Yeah. I've seen her get very angry. Not at co-workers but at situations." She does not yell. She's more apt to slam something. Once a phone was broken. The accountant laughs, and adds that her boss, who pays well, expects overtime hours from employees.

> **What is the best use of my time at the moment?**

Secretary Ginger Hedrick on her boss: "She's extremely sharp. It amazes me. If someone asks me a question, I'll have to think about it. But Mrs. Esty has the answer right away. Fast, sharp. She's self-confident, she's experienced." In business. And in life. "I have learned so much from her." Esty will explain her rationale if someone disagrees with her, but will become irritated and impatient if she explains several times and the person cannot understand. Does Mrs. Esty have a good memory? "Extremely." Ms. Hedrick sees only one fault: Esty does not give enough positive reinforcement.

The carpeted secretary's area is on the second floor, along with the other offices. Downstairs are the shipping room, quality-control area, testing, service, and calibration department, where check-out boards, sub-chassis, printed circuits, nodules, and other paraphernalia are being worked on. Neomed's shipping boxes state on the side "THE FINEST IN ELECTROSURGERY EQUIPMENT: NEOMED."

One employee who works on the first floor is Nedra Dearholt, Esty's mother, who talks of her daughter: "Janet was always much as she is now. . . . She used to get up at six o'clock to practice the flute before anyone else was up. When she was in 4-H, she won a science award for experimenting with white rats she kept in her bedroom. . . . Jan was the type that kept every piece of literature that she ever got . . . even newspapers. The shelves of her closet were packed with literature. . . ."

Her mother doubts her daughter will marry again. (Barbara

Hardy also cannot imagine her boss remarrying: "I don't think she needs it. I think her business is fulfillment enough.") Mrs. Dearholt sees Esty as a happy person. "Yes. I really think she is. . . . She can get *so* excited about something that's new and innovative. . . . She's someone who does what she wants to do, a self-motivator, an achiever." Dearholt lives in Boulder, not far from her daughter and granddaughter.

Andrea Esty—dreamy voice, long blond hair, thin wispy figure, nothing like her mother—describes Janet Esty as steadfast. "She's very, very ambitious and enjoys working. Really enjoys it. . . . She loves what she is doing. She forces me to be really independent." Although Andrea has her differences with her mother, she acknowledges her friends "think Mom's great." While she admires her determination, "I get kind of trapped in it, you know. Her whole life is that company. She loves it. She's crazy about it. I mean, she may not say it but I see it." The daughter—complaining about the usual lack of communication between herself and her mother—says, "We'll never really get down and talk." When Esty has a bad day at the office, "I get the butt end of it."

If she wasn't your mother, would you like her? "Yeah. I have deep respect for her." And she smiles and adds they "get crazy together and get into these little play-fights where we tickle each other and end up getting into weird conversations. Not like you'd expect mothers and daughters to get into. . . . I think we're good friends."

Mrs. Dearholt and Andrea are almost her whole social life. Esty says there aren't any males in her life today that are serious; her daughter remembers a man her mother was "really in love with . . . he was really good to me." And another who got killed in an auto accident after her mother rejected him; they went to his funeral, where, she says, Esty "caught all sorts of flack. They blamed her for his death. I saw a part of her that I had never seen before . . . frantic. Just *so* upset. I've *never* seen her that upset. It was horrible. I didn't like to see it . . . it was like seeing her at the very lowest point."

The hidden soft side of Esty revealed. Janet—with her businessman-image—is affectionate. A human being with an enthusiasm for life. And labor. Since high school, Janet Dearholt Esty has known nothing but work. Today she enjoys hustling, organizing, creating, maneuvering. An employee says she works 90 percent of her waking hours. For Esty that's perfect.

Question: What would you like to have written on your tombstone?

Esty: "I'd like not to have one."

7

THE FLYING "R"

Jean Rich

———◦⧔◦———

"WHEN I WENT to purchase a plane in Arizona, I took my tape recorder. And here I am with the president of the airline and the vice-president and everybody else [her voice quickens as she gains momentum], and I put the recorder in the middle of the table. And they looked at me so funny, you know? And they said, 'What are you doing?' And I said, 'Well, I want to make sure that everything is recorded so that we don't make mistakes.'" Jean Rich* adds, in her tiny shaky voice, the airline-industry executives never dealt with a woman at this level, and assumed the recording technique was some feminine twist. They were startled: "'You do that all the time?' they asked. I said, 'I want to make sure everything's done exactly the way we discussed.'" It was.

Jean Rich is five feet two (weight 114 pounds), with a dusky complexion and a head of deep brown curls. She was born in the late thirties in Lima to David Sanquesa, a Castilian Canadian, and Louisa Roggero, a Peruvian, whose expectations for her

---

*No relationship to the author.

rough-and-tumble daughter included the traditional roles of wife and mother, not director, president, treasurer, and general manager of Rich International Airways.

The Sanquesas had two children after Jean was born: a son two years after their daughter's birth, and Jacqueline about nine years later. The Sanquesas still act like honeymooners, according to Jean. "They go dancing on weekends; they're very young." Another child describes Mrs. Sanquesa as an easygoing settled woman who is happy to be at home; their children agree they are an attractive and affectionate couple.

David Sanquesa left Montreal at sixteen and, when his offspring were born, was in the aviation field. A maintenance man, he moved his family from Peru, when Jean was four, to Bolivia, then back to Lima, and finally all over South and Central America. As the family relocated, they regularly vacationed in Miami or New Orleans; in 1948 the Sanquesas moved to the United States permanently.

Jean never played with dolls, but enjoyed fishing with her father on weekends. "I was very close to—especially—my dad." Mr. Sanquesa states, "We were kind of strict parents, very strict parents," and adds Jean was close to them "up until a certain age, when she became more independent."

Jean—who today retains a childlike voice, with a resonance reminiscent of Joan Baez's—attended schools in the Miami area and at Coral Gables High. "I loved modern dance. . . . I was active in clubs, Debs Junior, Spanish National Honor Society, Student Council. I wasn't allowed to date." Fascinated with chess—"I learned how to play when I was a little girl"—she enjoyed volleyball and bicycle racing. As a teen, she was intrigued with stocks, bonds, and realty. "I dropped my interest in the stock market but real estate fascinates me. I still mess around with it."

After graduation from high school and general business courses

at a local school, she became a secretary at a small aircraft company. Continuing to live at home and adhering to her parents'
rules, the eighteen-year-old worked in the office position, began
learning the business, and met an older man, Homer Rich. A
family member says Jean attracts men with her "magnetism."

Three weeks after meeting Homer Rich, she eloped. Homer
was a test-pilot/inspector; Jean says he was handsome, and "I
don't know what possessed me. I think I was brought up too strict
and everything was a no-no. . . . All my girl friends had so much
freedom. [Her sister recalls Jean had to be in at ten on weekends.]
Maybe I decided, 'The heck with this. Maybe it's better if you're
married.' . . . All I can tell you is I took off and got married, and
that was it. . . in Macon [Georgia]." They left to marry on a
Friday night in 1955, and she was at work the following Monday,
scared to tell her parents. "My darn sister found the wedding rings
in the glove compartment of the car." The Sanquesas told their
oldest child, "You've made your bed. Now lie in it."

The marriage was rocky from the beginning. Jean's sister Jackie
got along with her new brother-in-law. "I was probably the only
one that did." Including Jean? "Right." Jackie Sanquesa
McGuire remembers Homer Rich often "going off on one of his
wild tangents. . . . We all had tempers," and she adds that Jean's
"flares up quite easily. It's a little harder to control than most."
After Jean and Homer's first serious fight, Jean's parents said that
as a married woman she must solve problems herself. She never
approached them with marital difficulties again. "That was it."

The Riches moved to New Jersey where Homer had a traveling
job with an aviation company. Jean's first two babies arrived
fourteen months apart: "Here I'm pregnant, and this business of
me being alone all the time. . ." She does not finish the sentence. "He worked hard. . . . I'll never forget calling my parents
on Christmas Eve from his office because I was helping him.
Those things affect a young girl."

After a few years, the couple moved back to the Miami area and started a fixed base operation at Tamiami Airport, including aircraft rentals and sales, chartering, light maintenance, parking for private planes, and flying-club facilities. An excellent salesperson, Jean was fascinated with business. She began to save her commission checks. At the same time, her interest in the stock market became more intense; she wished to train in New York for six months as a broker, "but," she says, "my husband didn't want me to."

The young mother continued to sell successfully from 1962 until 1964 while her husband traveled, and they fought. She remembers running the business and handling her two tiny children: "I even fueled airplanes. . . . Someone had to be there seven days a week." On weekdays she often took her babies to the airfield; when she left them with her mother weekends, she would still go back to have lunch with them. "I was running everything. I didn't have a maid or anything. . . . It was too much. I tended to worry too much about everything."

Her sister says, Jean "was burdened down with children, and no help. And worked with her husband as well. . . . I think she lost out on happiness along the way. I wish she had had more time for her children."

"I honestly don't know," says Jean when asked why her able, aggressive husband decided to sell the Miami business and go into consulting. He also became the circulation manager for a regional aviation magazine. "I was helping him out, doing all his translating, typing his letters. . . ." As he again changed jobs to another airline, Jean Rich became pregnant for the third time.

Life with Homer Rich was hectic. Jean says, "I couldn't keep up with his pace even though I'm very, very energetic. . . . I think it was too much for me." After her fourth pregnancy she decided the separation of that time would be a permanent one. "He wanted to make up again but it was too late. You forget [the hurt] so many times that after a while you just know that it is going to be the end of you. And you don't want your children to suffer. . . . I just thought I better try it on my own. And I really didn't know how I was going to do it."

Question: Do you ever wish you hadn't gotten married so early?

Answer: "No. I think I did the right thing. . . . Although it didn't work out. He was a very intelligent man and I was maybe too innocent, too young. . . . We were complete opposites."

At the time of her divorce in 1969, after fourteen years of marriage, she was mother to Linda, twelve; David, eleven; Steven, two; and Michael, nine months. Homer was so bitter that he never provided child-support. And she never wanted it.

Immediately after the divorce she went into business. "I had to. I mean, what was I going to live on? I mean I wasn't going to run to Mommy and Daddy." Her sister says: "The main thing that generated Jean was that she had to do something to raise her family. My father didn't believe in the liberated woman and that [Jean] could start a business on her own, and felt that she should go back to being a secretary . . . and she just had that fire in her to want to do it. . . . There were people who said she couldn't do it. She had to prove it not only to herself but to others."

Jean Rich decided to organize her own airline, utilizing bank loans and money saved from the years she sold airplanes between bearing and caring for babies. She traveled to Illinois to try to purchase a C-46 repossessed by a Chicago bank; she convinced the bankers to give her a huge unsecured mortgage. The aircraft was purchased for $50,000. Today its value is $119,000–$123,000. "C-46s are workhorses," comments Rich. With a certificate from the Federal Aviation Agency to carry cargo, she secured a contract and hired a captain and a co-pilot. The three overhauled the run-down plane in rented space. And she began working seven days a week: "When I started working full-time, I got a woman to live in. That woman is still with me. . . . Ana. She was so great. She was so good to me. Without her . . . The main thing was she loved the kids. I could never have gone out at night to work with the airplane. . . ." Jackie says, "She had to spend a lot of time away from her brood" throughout her marriage and after, and "I think they . . . resent that she didn't have the time for them." At some point, as the business was forming, Ana went to her native Nicaragua and Jean's mother again helped with the children. Jean dropped them in the morning and picked them up at the end of the day, which, she says, "was extremely hard on me. Ahhh. It was so tiring. It was very, very hard for me."

One of her first two employees was a pilot, well versed in maintenance, named William Meenan, who had previously worked as an airline captain for Homer Rich; "but I hardly knew him," says Jean. She tentatively hired someone else, who was killed in Puerto Rico just before he started. She says, "And Bill was working there [for Homer Rich]. He was very knowledgeable. And I used to say 'Hello'; you know how you talk to everybody. . . . And I guess I . . . ah . . . offered him a job. It occurred to me, 'How am I going to do this without people? I need a pilot and a co-pilot.' And that is how the airline got started going. With his help." Meenan had the necessary A. & P. (airframe and power plant) license to work on the plane, and also a pilot's license. "We were there night and day at the beginning. It was extremely hard," remembers Jean. "It was quite a bit of work, believe me. She explains the cargo-hauling business: "I sell service. When I tell them we'll be there at nine, we're in there at nine. Very punctual . . . We get the cargo in on time and undamaged. The people know we are reliable. So they call me. I think you have to have a good reputation with a name behind it [said backwards, characteristically]."

In her little singsong voice, with mixed accents of South America, south Florida, and some unplaceable additions, she remembers her first C-46, and points to its picture hanging on the wall behind her desk, carrying 14,000 pounds to the Bahamas, exactly what she needed for her first contracts, Winn-Dixie and Harvest Supermarkets. And then the Miami *Herald*. She transported that newspaper, the *New York Times*, and the *Wall Street Journal* to the Caribbean. "I lost one airplane. It wasn't amusing. It went into the ocean. Well, I guess the gentleman [the pilot] did not fuel, even though he was told to and he had eighteen hundred dollars in cash to do it. And by three-thirty I was calling Puerto Rico to see if my plane had arrived. I always check to see. And no sight of my plane. At twenty of four I got a telephone call . . . it was the captain. 'Oh, Jean! I've got bad news.' He landed in the water! A half-mile off the shore! It was the most *beautiful* airplane with an extra-large door. *Brand-new engines*. And he had the colossal nerve to say the engines conked out on him, that they had failed." She adds ironically that they did fail, "but of fuel exhaustion. We let him go immediately." This was her second plane. "I'll never forget that. It hit me like a ton of bricks." The aircraft was heavily financed. Jean managed to double her contracts to counteract this financial disaster.

Since then, her planes—"with the big blue 'R' on the tail"— have carried some odd cargo. Oil-well pipe to South America, lobsters, hazardous materials. Rich International took safari animals to Puerto Rico, "giraffes, buffaloes, lions—you name it. We had them in the airplane. They [the airport workers] let them down the ramp and the buffaloes went wild. In the airport. In Puerto Rico. *Voom!* They had to close the airport until the buffaloes were rustled up."

And Howard Hughes's belongings. "And nobody could know

about it. We flew his bed—his famous bed—and the boxes with the water he used to drink. It came from Nevada, and he only used a certain brand of paper towels." She moved his possessions from Nassau and was asked to oversee the move to Freeport personally.

Rich flew forty flights for the producers of the George C. Scott movie *The Day of the Dolphin.* She took their dolphins ("Fish. Not football players") to Nassau, and has handled Flipper. "We take the dolphins all over, all the time. In stretchers, in the water." Rich handles Miami Seaquarium cargo and Jacques Cousteau's gear. "We specialize in explosives. As long as you know what you're doing . . ." She has flown in the planes with the explosives, and casually compares the risk to city driving.

The only passengers she presently carries are military personnel and dependents as she moves a military installation to the Caribbean, a job that will take twelve months and cost over a million dollars. "It's a nice contract." She also does business with the Coast Guard and NASA, and with Central and South American corporations.

When she started in 1970, she was a private carrier and explains she could conceivably have flown an unsafe plane taking someone's property with her. "Then I got enough money to become a 121 Commercial Operator," regulated by the government to carry cargo. To be awarded this certification, a business must have a fixed amount of assets, indicate financial ability to maintain the planes properly, and generally run a safe airline.

In 1976, Rich International Airways became a supplemental air carrier. Her license—"I think it's the only one that's been given in a decade"—allows her to consolidate cargo, a savings for the customer. Previously she could only accept contracts which chartered the whole plane.

In 1977, Rich International became the only "dually certified" airline in America. That is, in addition to her supplemental status, which allows her planes to be chartered to points in Canada, the United States, the Caribbean, Mexico, Central and South America, she is also certified to fly to the Bahamas, and Turks' and Caicos Islands. The airline's unique status is "quite a thrill," says Rich proudly.

With careful attention to schedules and deadlines and clever competitive bidding, Rich's airline prospered. Today she has four DC-6s, three C-46s, and is "pretty sure we'll be going into jets." In addition to the air cargo service, Rich continues to buy and sell used planes.

Rich International Airways headquarters are located at the Miami International Airport in a white concrete one-story building, with full angled Caribbean-style shutters obscuring the interior view. A sign proclaims, in royal blue and white, "RICH INTERNATIONAL AIRWAYS." At the airport she has 9,300 square feet of ramp space leased from Pan American, a warehouse, plane wash rack, and a fixed base operation where space is rented to private businesses, corporations, and some banks; Rich also rents offices to a government agency on the other side of the field, "Kind of a quiet thing."

In her unpretentious office, with wooden sheet paneling on the walls, planes are heard constantly overhead. Pictures on her walls include Rich and Cousteau and several of her blue-and-white planes. Her desk has numerous thick piles of papers. "Usually I have everything spread all over and I know where to grab anything."

Bill Meenan, still an employee in charge of maintenance, spends most of his time on the field but walks in to confer with her on occasion. They discuss interior colors of a plane. "It has to be a very, very subdued white headliner," directs Rich. She looks at him and adds, "I'll have to go there and take care of it myself."

U. S. Federal Aviation Authority official J. Purcell congratulates Jean Rich—with husband Bill Meenan, smiling behind—as she becomes the president of an officially certified U. S. airline

Glancing at Meenan, Rich says, "I started up as a single girl and ended as a married woman." Shortly after the airline's organization, Meenan—a quiet, pleasant-looking man—and Jean Rich decided to marry. "We took off in our usual state for the airport, a half-hour late for the flight," states Jean, and Bill adds, in his soft, calm voice: "We were exhausted and we knew if we were to marry here, we'd be at work the next morning. So we took off. . . ." They flew to Jacksonville, rented a car, and drove to Georgia where they could wed quickly. "My family knew. My children knew," states Jean. But few others were aware of the marriage, according to the Meenans.

Meenan, extremely tall (he dwarfs his wife), states they operate independently. "In other words, a lot of people who speak to Jean don't realize I'm around." At work. "Right. It's no one's business." Jean, who is never known as Mrs. Meenan, says "our private life is so private" that the people they work with are not aware they are married. "We keep it separate." Employees do know they live together, however. "Oh, yeah, they see us walking in together," states Meenan. Everyone knows they have the same home telephone number. He adds: "We really haven't tried to keep it a big secret. On the other hand, we haven't gone around talking about it. . . . People might think, Oh, she's shacking up with him. We have never hidden the fact that we are together, we live together. . . . There may be a lot of people running around with the wrong idea. . . . Who cares?" His wife adds, properly, "I think the people who know me and Bill know that we are fairly straight. . . . I always carry my wedding band with me." (Jackie, commenting on the covert marriage: "I can't tell you why. I don't understand it. I've always been puzzled by it.") Bill concedes, "Maybe a lot more people know than we realize. . . . We didn't start married, so I think it's not good policy for people to know now that we're married. We've been running it pretty good." No one can argue with that point.

Meenan, as covert husband of the boss, has overheard co-employees remarking: "What's a woman doing in a position like that?" He comments: "I think a lot of men feel a woman doesn't have any business in aviation." Adds his wife: "They don't think a woman can make it. And I have been told that personally. . . . Well, if a man can run it, I believe a woman can. And I'm *doing* it. And I'm doing it successfully. . . . In aviation especially, it's tough. Very tough to be a female, much less a woman boss. You should advise women planning to be in any sort of business that it is rough on their husbands, I think." But a woman—like a man—needs practical and emotional help: "You need support, but you can get it from an employee, an interested party . . . *or* a husband. . . . But if I had to do it totally on my own—and I *did* do it on my own—I mean *I* had to come up with the ideas, *I* had to think of the money in the beginning. It was all *me*. But certainly a husband or friend or whatever is a great help. You need support . . . not only from him but from everyone around you. But *I* made it; I am the first U.S. woman president of a certificated airline. . . . I am the *only* one, according to the Federal Aviation."

With separate functions in the business—she sells, handles business and contracts, and he oversees maintenance—being the boss's spouse "doesn't interfere at all," says Meenan, because (1) he does not like business or sales, (2) most people don't even know he is her husband, and (3) he is not interested in promotion. He begins to expound as she interjects, "He's very quiet. He doesn't want to talk to people . . . not the outgoing talkative type." Waiting until she is through, he continues his sentence where he was interrupted. " . . . and I'm always amazed at the nothing conversations that salesmen go through. It's not really my area of interest." He adds that he's watched Jean do it several times. She says, obviously delighted, "He thinks my technique's unbelievable. Remember you're dealing with a lot of people and you have to give these people an answer, one which is not a lie but which is also something—" For once, he interrupts her: "It's been called 'the fine art of negotiation.'" Jean: "Well, I've been called something else but I'm not going to say it," and comments they are opposites. I'm a Capricorn. Capricorns are very business-minded. . . . My husband's a Libra. They're stubborn. Very quiet but stubborn. They say that Libras balance a Capricorn."

Meenan—a subdued long-limbed stoic individual, with a set smile and a quiet immutability—discusses the situation of being an employee of Jean Rich's: "Well I'll tell you the truth. If I have to work for someone, I don't think I could ask for any better working conditions. She's the boss. I don't think I would rather work for anyone else. I'm sure people wonder, How can you work for your wife? How can you hack it? But I enjoy it—" Jean interrupts: "That's because you make a lot of the decisions." Her comment is ignored as he continues: "I admire Jean's decision-making ability. I think that she makes good, sound decisions and I think that she has good, sound policies and I couldn't fault them. A lot of time she makes a decision when I have trouble making up my mind. And a lot of time I'm grateful for it. I'm glad I didn't have to make that decision." "He's a thinker and he's got to have time," she says, while she makes snap decisions. But sometimes isn't it better to think things out more thoroughly? "I don't think I've made a mistake yet! Have I? I haven't made a mistake yet," Rich counters aggressively. Meenan: "I don't think you've made any *major* mistakes." His voice is almost inaudible. Rich explains that in the aviation business immediate decisions—within an hour, generally—must be made. Planes must land and depart on schedule, with no time for deep consideration.

Yet at home she takes forever to reach a decision. Hours are spent deciding upon draperies or clothes, but, says Meenan, "That's a different Jean. The funny part of it is, she wishes she had someone who was her size to take care of her clothes problems for her." Her trim figure belies the fact that she has four children, two now adults. Often she wears the hand-me-downs of her sister, who is in the women's-wear business. Meenan states his wife can afford anything she wants, "And you go out and put your sister's clothes on!" When she goes shopping, she often takes Meenan, who complains, "I can't stand to shop." At Christmas, she orders from Neiman-Marcus, Saks, Burdine's, and Jordan Marsh catalogues exclusively.

Rich's two elder children have left home: her son David is a college student, and daughter Linda, a model, married at eighteen and has made her young mother a grandma. The Meenans live in their South Miami home with the housekeeper Ana, who returned from South America to her old job, and the two boys (who call Meenan "Dad") from Homer Rich's and Jean's marriage. In an upper-middle-class neighborhood, their unglamorous home with pool does not seem particularly fitting for the well-to-do wife—with the exception of Rich's newly decorated bathroom. Of Italian marble—including the custom-made tub with two steps leading to it—this room, with walls and ceilings fully lined by mirrors, has fourteen-carat-gold sink faucets and spigots. A separate room houses the toilet and shower stall. On the floor in front of the stall is a bath mat proclaiming "Waldorf-Astoria."

In addition to the home, this youthful woman with a small voice and large drive owns a condominium for her personal use: "I like to walk down the beach. I love the ocean. I love Key Biscayne." Owner of four expensive Commodore Club apartments, she sold two at a profit. Real estate is "great on Key Biscayne. I'm making more and more money." In the Key Biscayne Marina, their inboard-outboard Bertram-25 is moored. When does she use the condominium? "On weekends I'll go." Alone? "No. I'll take him [her husband] with me." The children stay with their housekeeper. "Oh, yeah. It's my hideaway." Meenan smiles.

The condominium—furnished in *nouveau-riche*—overlooks

Biscayne Bay, with a view of the subtropical sunset. Its lobby is expensively decorated and it is considered to be one of the plushest buildings in the area.

Rich also rents houses and apartments. When she first became a landlord, she cleaned and made repairs herself. "I don't have to do that any more."

Aside from real-estate investments, Rich likes to buy expensive dogs. She and Meenan own an Irish wolfhound and a German shepherd. "I gave him all my animals," states Rich about her husband, implying he is in charge of their care. "That's it," he concurs. She ordered her Irish wolfhound from Ireland, and says the dog's name is Wolf; her husband disagrees. He says his name is Woof. Rich looks at Meenan with astonishment: "I call him *Wolf* and you call him something else?" Meenan: "Woof." Rich: "Are you kidding me?" Meenan: "You know, like 'woof, woof.'" Rich: "Bill, since when? You're unbelievable. You're losing your marbles." The wolfhound stands taller than a Great Dane. "I don't know what the heck possessed me to get a dog like that. I gave it to Bill." Absolving all responsibility.

Along with dog purchases, Rich buys antique jewelry. Diamonds. "She doesn't wear it but she loves it," states Meenan, and she enjoys purchasing handmade jewelry, gold with diamonds and emeralds, and pearls. She wears a Capricorn necklace inscribed "Happy Anniversary, All my love."

Rich works hard by day, and relaxes with music at night: Chopin, Wagner, *La Traviata*, *Carmen*, *Madame Butterfly*, *The Mikado*. "I like dancing but my husband is not a dancer. I dance by myself." As they recall her dancing to "that jungle beat," as she describes it, they giggle privately. It is suggested perhaps she does her dancing in the mirrored bathroom. Meenan laughs softly: "Well, I think at home you're a woman and—" She finishes his sentence, "And at work I'm a woman." A woman in the house and a woman as boss.

Question: Is Jean logical or erratic? Is she moody, easygoing? How would you describe her?

Answer: "All of the above. There are different Jeans. There's the home Jean, there's the work Jean, and I think really she has achieved something that I'll never be able to achieve, at least not to any great degree. She can turn the office on and off at will. I can't. It's like she has a switch. I can't do that. But she can be at home and the business phone will ring and she'll do business. When the business is over, she transfers to whatever she was doing before the call. And I can't do that. I fume and sputter and bark." It is hard to imagine this mild-mannered man raising a fuss. He thinks for a few seconds, and adds, "I think she really *is* all of the above. When she is a woman, she is as illogical as a woman can be. And when she's a businesswoman she's as logical and calculating as a businessman needs to be."

Rich believes that when you go home you must be with your family and communicate with them. "I'm a firm believer in this." She does not encourage social relationships with people who discuss airplanes. "At nighttime I like to read, or watch TV once in a while. My daughter thinks I'm old-fashioned. I like to see old movies. . . ." She enjoys Barbara Walters, documentaries. Invited to Senators' dinners, particularly ones connected with aviation regulation or lobbying, she usually declines. "I just like to be with my children. Bill and I like to go out on the boat, take the kids and go fishing. . . ." A close unpretentious family: Rich cuts her husband's hair because it's practical and convenient.

Meenan says his wife is practical to the point where it annoys him. "If something bothers her, you'll know it." He turns to her: "You're very explosive." She demands inarticulately, "I'd like to know what?" and starts interrogating him.

Her strength and her argumentativeness, stubbornness, and

impatience are almost invisible because she has that little voice: "I answer the phone and they say, 'Can I talk to your mommy, please?'" But if something is said that she disagrees with, she will let it be known.

As a child, according to her father, "she had her temper and her own way of doing things. . . . She always wanted her way." She admits she expresses anger. "I'm not gonna whisper to 'em. I've got a Spanish background. They say that's temperamental. . . ."

Her voice, choice of words, temperament, and appearance do not suggest her intrinsic intelligence and *fuerza*. Yet the stride of this little girl-woman with flashing dark eyes is sure; her self-confidence is evident in her relationship with friends, husbands, interviewers, maître d's. Airline-industry people—competitors—admit they have a great deal of respect for her: "She is quite a dynamic woman."

Her father expected his oldest child to marry and have children. She surprised him. "Definitely." She is not astonished, and is proud of her achievements—"I am. Believe me, I am"—as she again explains, "I couldn't—to support my children—be a secretary. You know you don't make enough money as a secretary. I had been used to running my husband's business. I knew I could make money on my own. So I decided, 'What the hell, I can make it or break it. . . .' I had to gamble. It was a good gamble."

Rich's father considers her a workaholic. When asked about his statement as she considered trying the aviation business—that she couldn't "hack it"—he defends himself: "Well, I didn't say it *that* way. I said it was kind of a jungle, this kind of work, and I didn't think she'd be able to handle it, is all. . . . Well, you can't be right *all* the time."

8

AN UNDERSTATEMENT
OF HERSELF

Beverly Willis

———⋅⋅⟨∞⟩⋅⋅———

SHE WAS twenty-six years old when she designed the interior of
the Shell Bar in Henry Kaiser's new Honolulu hotel. Beverly
Ann Willis was just entering the world of architecture when,
more than two decades ago, industrialist Kaiser announced he
liked the Willis touch in his cocktail lounge. He was not as
pleased with the landscape architect's creation: "So Kaiser decided that he and I were going to design a garden. Well, I had
never designed a garden in my life and neither had Henry Kaiser,
to the best of my knowledge. . . . It was an experience that has
been with me the rest of my life. Henry Kaiser operated by saying
to you that he doesn't expect you to know everything. He understands there are things you might not know. He does, however,
expect you to be very honest with him. If you don't know, you are
expected to say, 'I don't know.' But you *are* expected to know
where you can find the answer. And you're supposed to find

it. . . . The theory is you go out to the site itself [to create the design], so we had a little thirty- by forty-inch table right there overlooking the garden we were going to design. . . . Along with the table . . . comes a telephone. I can't remember *how* long the cord was. . . ." As they walked through the flower beds and shrubbery mentally relocating them, Beverly Willis, often baffled, used the telephone to obtain the instant answers demanded by the eighty-two-year-old man beside her. "I *still* don't know the names of the plants! Neither of us knew. It was the blind leading the blind. That afternoon, the construction crew moved in. It was done for opening night, the day after." The year was 1955. Miss Willis clarifies her position today: "I do not represent myself as a landscape architect."

Beverly Ann Willis does represent herself as an architect. This Westerner—born in Tulsa, reared in Portland, Oregon—was, at one time or another, a newspaper artist, a columnist, an auto-supply stock girl, a soda jerk, a drugstore clerk, a gas-station tire-changer, a riveter, a craftsperson, a welder, a muralist, a meat-packer, a sculptress, furniture-maker; an interior decorator . . . and, on that one occasion, a landscape architect.

When she started at Oregon State University, however, she wanted to be an engineer. Willis became editor of the school newspaper and also wrote a college column, "Willy Nilly," for the Portland *Oregonian* newspaper, where she worked as a tour guide. As she learned about printing and continued to write, she slowly realized engineering was not for her.

Fascinated with the printing business and graphic-related processes, she obtained employment at a lithography plant and attended night school to learn more. While she supported herself free-lancing in the graphics field, she moved to San Francisco, began to paint creatively as well, and found she loved it.

A one-person show of Willis paintings at Sutter Street's prestigious Maxwell Galleries, in San Francisco, was followed by an invitation from a television station to teach watercolor painting on camera. "Everyone commented on how Oriental my work was. . . ." Chinese friends looked at her creations and mentioned a Buddhist influence.

Willis, a self-proclaimed "great believer in following clues," decided to re-enter college and study Far Eastern art; she selected the University of Hawaii as the place in the United States to learn of Oriental creativity. This choice was a "great milestone" in her life; "the inner turmoil" stopped and she was at peace with herself. The mental calm she found when she entered the University of Hawaii followed what she refers to, in her pleasant deep-toned voice, as "the painful problem of growing up."

Willis's mother, Margaret Porter, married Lagrand Willis, member of an established clan in Broken Bow, Nebraska. Lagrand, who shared a total of twenty-one divorces with his five brothers, inherited the family land when the brothers all died of heart attacks before the age of fifty. Says Beverly, "My father's been married five times. . . . This was before it was popular. . . ."

The Willises were divorced when Beverly was six and, until she was fifteen, she saw her father once. Before the breakup, the family traveled from one town to another as Lagrand worked at oil sites. Afterward, Beverly, her brother Ralph, and their mother settled in Oklahoma City, then later moved to Portland.

Since Lagrand Willis supported them neither financially nor emotionally, Mrs. Willis, a nurse, earned money for food and clothes for the essentially fatherless children, and for her children's schooling.

Shortly after the divorce, Mrs. Willis decided to send her daughter and son to a parochial boarding school. They stayed there for several years, including the summers. For the next nine years, Beverly was *de facto* a child without a family. The adult

Beverly defends her mother's decision: "She felt it was better that we had a good education. She didn't feel she could work and take care of us, watch over us. . . . Basically, a Catholic boarding school is very good. . . . I learned to put sentences together and spell and all those good things. . . . I didn't like it, but her line of reasoning was pretty solid."

Question: But you missed other things, emotional things, didn't you?

Answer: "Yes. But I look at a lot of other people, and at least I got a good education. . . . I was clearly on my own. It was a great asset. I *hated* it; I felt so sorry for myself as a kid. There was nothing I wanted more than a normal family and a home to live in, instead of that boarding school. All the kids really had them, and I really sort of felt I was being discriminated against. . . . But now I've grown older and I look back and I really say, 'Thank God!' "

While she was in boarding school, until the age of fifteen, she believes her mother married and divorced two or three times. . . . Mrs. Willis says, "No, she's mixed up there. I had one husband [Beverly's father]." When asked if perhaps Margaret Willis had boyfriends her daughter thought were husbands, she says, "Yes, I think so. Um-huh." (Beverly Willis claims her father was Margaret Willis's second husband. Mrs. Willis says he was the only one.)

Beverly's absent father continued to marry, sire offspring, and divorce. Beverly does not know his total child-count. "I really don't have that much contact. . . ." Familiarity with other relatives is even skimpier. "I have a vague memory of meeting a grandparent, but my conscious memory says I've never met either of my grandparents—*any* of my grandparents." Mrs. Willis says, "She met her grandfather, but I don't think she recollects it. . . ." What about aunts, uncles? Did Mrs. Willis have siblings?

Beverly says, "Oh, not that I know of. . . . My mother just never liked talking about her family. I have never known anything about her family." (Mrs. Willis had a sister.)

At the age of fifteen, Beverly went home to live, stayed with her mother for a short time, then decided to leave. Mrs. Willis agreed. "My mother, I think, felt I was too much for her to handle. . . . She made a very wise decision. Because if my mother had attempted to hold me down, I probably wouldn't be speaking to her today. . . . I was really quite capable of taking care of myself at an extraordinarily early age." Supporting herself with part-time jobs, she lived in a rooming house and attended high school, dropped out for a period of time, eventually graduated. While in high school, in addition to her part-time jobs, she was active in athletic activities. Mrs. Willis states, "She liked baseball; you couldn't keep her away." She was on a world-championship team when she was sixteen, playing shortstop and left field, and she also skied and was a long-distance swimmer. Of her teen years, Beverly comments, "Mine were particularly painful. . . . [I was] very unhappy because I was really confused. I didn't know what I wanted to be or do."

She applied to college and was accepted at Oregon State; Mrs. Willis paid the tuition. "But her money ran out," Beverly says, "and so then I started working my way through the rest of it." College was a new experience for her; for the first time, she had close friends and was popular. "I really had a ball in college." Beverly also had her first relationship with a man. "Probably if things had happened differently, I would have married." This was during the years after World War II when there were just a handful of women in the schools and thousands of men aged about twenty-three to fifty-five. A mature atmosphere pervaded the universities, and for the seventeen-year-old, inexperienced in close emotional relationships, it was confusing. This particular man was twenty-three, and had lived through the war as the sole survivor of three squadrons. "He was going through hell because of it," according to Beverly. "He finally married a woman he had known in Europe during the war, a European who was a little bit older than he. She had had some of the same experiences he did."

Beverly says a conscious decision was made then. She could not be happy hoping for or accepting the monetary protection of a man, a spouse. She did not want to be a reflection of any male. Her father "was sort of an independent guy," she says, "and I presume I take after him." She believes his lack of financial responsibility for her solidified her resolve to assure her own self-sufficiency.

Her determination was strong; the vehicle for reaching this goal was confused. After majoring in engineering for two years at Oregon State, she left college for three years, became involved in artistic endeavors, and applied and was accepted at the University of Hawaii. She moved to Honolulu.

In the Territory of Hawaii in 1952, Beverly Ann Willis met Louise Dillingham, her mentor. An old-line Hawaiian family who settled in the Islands in 1865, the Dillingham clan continues to be socially and financially powerful in the fiftieth state.

Louise Dillingham—in her seventies in '52—and Beverly Willis were college classmates and became friends in Hawaii. The resulting relationship between the elderly Dillingham and Beverly was perhaps one of the most important friendships in Beverly's life.

The Dillinghams' entertaining was a new experience for this young woman, who had no firsthand knowledge of the life of a lively, sociable family. Louise Dillingham knew, Beverly says, "If you have an attractive twenty-year-old and you put her in a room with sixty-year-old men, the sixty-year-old men love it." Willis today loves to throw parties, often following the Dillingham pattern of mixing age groups. As the Dillinghams' protégée, Beverly was introduced to people—people who mattered. "If the Dillinghams said you were the person for the job, that's all it took."

While the friendship developed, and during the years she attended the University of Hawaii, Beverly set up a pioneering crafts business, Willis Workshop. In this she included her brother Ralph, who worked with her on stucco bric-a-brac and also created plastic tables before use of that material was popular.

Hawaii was an excellent location for a fledgling go-getter. Since it was far from the mainland, creative and promising individuals were offered jobs and contracts by default; few truly qualified people were available. Willis says it became a situation of "Do you want to do it?"—with few questions regarding credentials. "All you really had to say was 'I would like to do it.'" Willis said that often. On the usual procedure of formally preparing yourself to be qualified to work in a new field, she says, "I didn't have to go through that in Hawaii"—pronouncing it "He-why," almost as one syllable.

Her relationship with the Dillinghams and her success with the Willis Workshop combined to make her a newsworthy individual. A full-page spread in the Honolulu paper described five 10' × 15' murals she painted to hang in the Royal Hawaiian Hotel, today displayed in Hawaii's United Chinese Society building; another piece featured her three-hundred-pound Tiki, carved for United Airlines, now in their Waikiki ticket lobby. "People on the street recognized me. . . . I've never received such notoriety since then."

Through Dillingham connections, the Henry Kaiser decorating job was offered to her. As she graduated with an art degree, Kaiser representatives commissioned her to redo the interior of the cocktail lounge—the Shell Bar—regularly used as a backdrop for the "Hawaii Five-O" television series. In addition to choosing the wall coverings, flooring, and ceilings, she designed original furniture and the bar itself. The garden-landscaping job followed, with Kaiser by her side. She recalls that when the Kaiser Shell Bar and then the garden project offers were made, "I did it. Never had done it before. But then that's the story of my life." She assumed she could handle the challenge. A substantial designing concern grew from her Willis Workshop and Kaiser-related jobs, aided by another of her first clients after graduation, Admiral Felix Stump.

A five-star admiral in charge of the Pacific armed forces, Stump engaged her to redo his headquarters. Satisfied, he then awarded her a contract to design officers' clubs, normally a Corps of Engineers project. However, these particular facilities were for men accustomed to lavish Tokyo accommodations, including slot machines and geisha girls. Willis had control and responsibility over contracting, engineering, designing, furnishing, carpeting—everything. While the Shell Bar at Kaiser's Hawaiian Village involved designing the interior and furnishings and the execution of the sand-sculpture mural behind the bar, she did not handle the contract for it, and did no architectural or engineering work. Admiral Stump's offer included all phases of the project.

By 1956, the Willis Workshop gave way to Willis & Associates. And occasionally her Honolulu firm employed architects. Willis was not licensed. However, as she watched the designers, she said to herself, "I can do this better than they're doing it," and, aided by engineering and mathematics courses taken at Oregon State, she observed and learned architecture and became well versed in construction techniques. She remembers hiring Oriental workers, who, testing her, would tell her on specific projects, "Me no know how." She showed them; in the end she could do the labor herself.

Although she was successful in the Territory, she recognized construction projects were limited there. Problems included minimal access to information about materials and a less sophisticated, slower pace. She was, she said, "looking for a bigger pond—and I found a bigger pond in San Francisco."

Her newly opened San Francisco business handled mainly residential work, but it gradually expanded into commercial projects, hospital and school design, and in the late 1960s she began to apply her talents to large-scale housing. With seed money from architectural projects, she invested in land, and her firm became a mixture of architectural services, urban landownership, real-estate planning and developing, and management. She explains, "I did not make money in architecture. I made money in property development. Basically there's not enough money in architecture to make money *at* it. . . . I've invested in property and property development. . . . I wouldn't want to give anyone the impression that you become an architect and make money."

The making of Beverly Willis—a square-browed wispy-blond-haired substantial woman in her late forties—is due in part to what she calls a "gutsy streak . . . the gambler instinct." In her slow Western twang, modified by years in Hawaii and California, she expounds that human beings, like animals, are trained in self-reliance. She says, "I don't think we're very far from the jungle, and I think we kid ourselves when we think we are. . . . Animals push their babies out. We must cut the umbilical cord and push children out. Let them work it out."

Beverly Willis was shoved out, managed to find her footing, and ultimately ended up the chief of a high-powered publicity-conscious architectural-design and land-management corporation in San Francisco.

"I think my mother's proud of me. . . . She's a very intelligent person," muses Beverly. Mrs. Willis says of her daughter, "She's

Beverly Ann Willis, Architect

been a very steady girl." Beverly harbors no ill-will toward her mother for foisting self-reliance on her as a young child; in fact she credits her parent for her foresight. When Willis was organizing her concern in San Francisco, her mother joined the firm as a bookkeeper. "For the first time, in San Francisco, I saw more of my mother than I had in my knowing life."

Mrs. Willis, now retired, lives in Anacortes, a little town in the state of Washington.

In that small hamlet, located on a peninsula sticking out into the waters above Puget Sound about halfway between Seattle and Vancouver, Margaret Willis became a late bloomer. She decided the town needed a bus service for the elderly, organized it, and raised funds, then located a senior citizen center building and secured an interest-free loan from the bank. Never a forceful person, she amazed her daughter as she became transformed at the age of sixty. "It was a 100-percent-different personality. A 180-degree turnaround. She was no longer intimidated, timid." Mrs. Willis lives alone, and is now a jewelry-crafter, goldsmith, and oil painter. Her daughter says, "I think my creativity definitely comes from my mother, although she did not learn to express herself until very late in life."

On one of a group of islands close to Anacortes—the San Juan Islands—is the home of Ralph ("Bud") Willis, Beverly's brother. He makes his own liquor and wine, and slaughters a steer once a year, utilizing the skin for jackets and gloves and freezing the meat. He has a sawmill and makes his own lumber. Mrs. Willis on her son: "He's sort of different. He's not as pushy as his sister." A friend says, "Bud's great. He's what you'd call your real country gentleman." Like Beverly, he never married.

Beverly Willis was tempted to wed several times. But was scared: "I have tremendous admiration and respect for women who can hold down an important job and be married, too, and have children. When I look back, I just don't see how I could have done what I have done and had those other responsibilities as well. On the other hand, you can argue it's a help. . . . You have support as well as responsibilities. . . . Of course most of my life is spent with men. I see very few women in my everyday life. . . ." Women seem to like Beverly. A New England friend, Dee Dee Gifford, feels she is shy, and pushes herself to be a public person; Beverly has told her she finds it hard to speak in public. Mrs. Gifford says Beverly has the capacity for close friendship, and sees her as a woman with no pretensions, "an understatement of herself." A male friend says she takes charge of things in an inoffensive way. She does not waste or mince words. With an easy smile, Willis never makes one feel exploited, according to another male acquaintance, who finds her "an attractive person, with a very good way with men."

She has a certain style, an unusual combination of simple tastes, affluence, and, unexpectedly, sophistication. Perhaps a bit shy, Willis still manages to handle herself well and at the same time make others in her presence immediately comfortable.

"I have a tremendous amount of energy, and I like to be on the move and I move very rapidly. . . . I let my steam out," says Willis, who yells when she is angry and cools off quickly. "I do not hold grudges. I sometimes see people harboring grudges and getting even six years later, but I don't have time for that."

Beverly Willis knows what she thinks, and states it. A dogmatic realist, she is sentimental. "Oh, I'm a real crybaby. [Deep-belly laughter.] I'm a real sentimental sort. . . . When I was a kid, I was ashamed to cry. . . . What the hell . . . It releases a lot of tension."

Though she is fond of children, she believes she would be an inadequate mother: "This is my observation; I have not done any research, et cetera [Willis says "et cetera" quite often], but it would be hard to convince me I'm not right. Women do not know how to be mothers without being taught. A good mother is trained by a good mother. . . . In my instance, I was separated. . . . I grew up in schools away from my mother, and of course away from my father."

She likes to socialize with young people in the role of teacher or guru. Her relationships with young adults and the ability to pull these people into her social realm came, she says, after "I went through that whole phase—which a lot of people do—when, in order to hide my insecurities, I was enormously aggressive." Still a forceful person, she can now spend an entire social evening speaking very little. But that was achieved over a period of time; "it didn't just happen."

In fact, nothing in Willis's life "just happened." With an air of healthy common sense, she says, "If you have the guts, you can do it. If you don't have the guts . . . What is it the Jewish people call it? *Chutzpah*. . . . It's motivation, drive; there's no question about that. But you also have to have a strange courage. . . . If there's a will, there's a way. If you really want it, you can do it. You've got to make up your own mind; do you want it or don't you want it?" Beverly Willis made her decision long ago. And being female made no difference. In fact, she feels a woman in architecture has an advantage. She notices people remember her "name and face, et cetera. If I were a man," she says, "I would have to meet them three or four times." She plans to utilize every advantage to make a substantial impression in the field of architecture, both nationally and internationally. "We have often been told that women just cannot do these things, that they're just not as talented as men, whether they're artists or musicians or what-have-you [another favorite expression]. I don't believe that. And I think it would be nice to be able to achieve the very top of the profession. And I'm very interested in doing that. God willing, I think I will."

Within her company, her partner, David Coldoff (a University of Toronto graduate in architecture), thinks she will because of her ability. He says, "People have said to me, 'I'm sure Beverly gets along with that client because she's a woman.' That's not my impression at all. Her relationship to clients has always been on a human-being-to-human-being basis. . . . I see no attempt ·to deliberately use the fact that she's a woman, and I don't see much in the clients' reaction that they see her as a woman, either. . . . They react to her as a professional in business." Friends and business associates ask what it is like working for a woman, but he never considers it on that level. He views her as a highly intelligent, organized, and innovative boss.

And the boss comments on construction workers' reaction to her: "Never had any problems. *Never.* Never in my life have I

Ms. Willis as hostess during a formal affair in her home

had any problem being a woman boss on a construction site or in an office."

Willis, accepted as a female, is active in women's organizations. With the Delegation for Friendship Among Women, she traveled with a group of seventeen to China. Earlier, in 1969, she went to the Soviet Union with several of the same delegates, then Rumania and Yugoslavia, meeting with Soviet women's committees. She often travels with her closest female companion, Joan Schisler, a neat, rounded St. Louis Junior Leaguer in her late twenties. Schisler is social secretary, assistant, and "woman for all seasons," in her words.

The competent Ms. Schisler, who has a hearty laugh much like Willis's, plans the architect's parties and purchases her clothing, and, she says, "Beverly has a Japanese housekeeper and . . . I run the household." Schisler has complimentary comments on her boss, friend, and apartment-mate, and states, "I'm sure this is a 'till death do us part situation.'" Wearing a gold band ring on her third finger, left hand, she explains, "I suppose it saves you a little bit of trouble sometimes when you don't really want to be bothered."

The two women, well tuned to each other, have similarities. Willis also wears a ring on the third finger of her left hand. "I don't consider it a wedding ring. I consider it a band ring. And I never even thought about it, as a matter of fact, until somebody said it looks like a wedding ring. I have very little jewelry." She doesn't care for it.

A dapper male associate comments, "I'm impressed by her taste. I like her style." Willis, with a weakness for fine shoes which she orders custom-made in Hong Kong, considers appearances and entertaining important: "I enjoy spending money. . . . I think the thing that perhaps I spend the most money on is entertaining. I enjoy entertaining. And the way I enjoy entertaining is an expensive way of entertaining...sometimes black-tie and sometimes not, depending upon the mood or the occasion, et cetera." Schisler says, "She has an extremely well-known social life." Loving the trappings of sociability, when she, however, accidentally drops food in her lap while eating, the sturdy five-foot-five Willis chuckles. "I never learned good manners. . . . I'm interested in eating." Then she picks up her napkin, dips it in her water glass, and cleans her clothes. Unpretentious.

A straightforward no-nonsense individual, Willis at times has esoteric leanings. On astrology: "I don't really believe in it," yet she adds, "I do tend to think that they have *captured* some basic characteristics of some basic types of people. I'm an Aquarius. . . ."

Beverly Willis lives in the top-floor flat located in a Willis-owned three-story building, with a view of San Francisco from the bedroom and the ocean and the city visible from the living room. In addition to her San Francisco antique-filled apartment, she owns a country place in the foothills of the Sierra Nevada. Willis bought an 1855 schoolhouse in the gold-rush town of Volcano. A one-room structure when it was purchased from the school district, she creatively converted it to a unique three-bedroom home with a corrugated-tin roof and a bell and belfry with an eagle on the top. Willis enjoys sitting on an unusual rock outcrop within her pool reading, with her dog relaxing in the water beside her.

Weekends are for pleasure. Business fills the other five days.

Beverly Ann Willis, licensed architect, considers herself "a generalist. . . . I have a substantial amount of creative ability in a wide range of fields, architecture actually being one, but painting and muraling and sculpturing [she laughs]. . . and a lot of crafts, et cetera. . . . In my mind, I'm a very creative person. I'm a very talented person. . . . I'm not a technician."

She is knowledgeable about technical matters, however. Although Willis's firm was not the first in computer work within
architecture, Miss Willis states she has an emerging reputation
in the sield, and she sees new communities "really needing"
comprehensive computerized programs. During a hundred-and-
fifteen-million-dollar Corps of Engineers housing project in
Hawaii—touted by Willis as the largest United States housing
project, built for a community of twelve thousand—Willis was
able to begin construction nine months from the day of con-
tract-signing, utilizing computerized cost analysis. This is a
national track record for this sort of thing; the sooner building
begins after bids, the more profitable the project, owing to rising
costs of materials and labor. Willis, concerned about design as
well as cost, observes, "Design has to be defined as something
that is architecturally pleasing—that, for sure—but it also must
meet functional and social and economic criteria. . . . A building
is in a sense a useful object. It's something that has a function,
like a teakettle . . . and it's got to do a job. And it's also got to do a
job within a certain cost. Or it's not economically feasible. . . . It's
got to relate in a practical way. I mean the elevators have got to
work and all that. But it also has to relate to people in a successful
way . . . which is why I've developed this humanistic philosophy
as a criterion for evaluating . . . whether a design is decent or
not." She wants people to be comfortable physically and
psychologically in her structures. "And emotionally." The pressure of society is, she thinks, stripping self-respect. High-rise
neighbors are strangers although they pass every day. Her solution: build an entryway servicing only six doors, and people will
get to know one another. She refers to this as "humanistic architecture," and it is exemplified in her prize-winning Nob Hill
Courts building at 930 Pine Street, San Francisco. The quiet
courtyard of Vine Terrace creates a feeling of serenity as the city

In her San Francisco offices, Willis confers with associates

Willis, in hard hat, on the job

sounds are muffled by the structure's walls.

"People buy," she says, "because that is what they think they should be doing, and they never stop to think, Well, what do I really like? How am I going to relate to my family in this space?" Willis says with chagrin that everyone worries about the spiraling cost of housing, but "when there is square footage in a home which is not used, you pay a hell of a lot of money for it, and you continue to pay for it all your life. . . ." She is irritated when people don't buy what they as human beings need, but instead purchase what is touted in a home magazine.

Her clients evidently like her philosophy; Willis's firm of thirty-five employees is steadily growing, with a one-year construction volume of two hundred and fifty million dollars. Willis & Associates, Inc. is run exactly as Beverly wishes. Impatient with plodding, careful, meticulous types, she says, she chose to "weed out the people who tend to be slow and methodical. . . . Not that they can't do every bit as good a job, but the pace of working has got to be compatible." And she is fast. Joan Schisler says her boss can do more work in an hour than anyone she knows.

Willis's offices are located in an old printing shop where large beams and pillars once held the weight of heavy printing presses. Bright blue dividers separate the office areas, and fabric wall hangings, antique wooden tools, and plants decorate the white walls and the exterior brick walls. In the far rear is the drafting area. Beverly's office—with her super-neat desk—is visible as one walks into the back section past the receptionist's desk.

She also has a Washington, D.C., office; her main business there involves a General Services Administration project for use by the Internal Revenue Service: a prototypical computer building to be built in nine different geographic sites throughout the country. Necessarily up-to-date in terms of safety, security, acoustics, illumination, and energy conservation, her design will be reused by the I.R.S. for the next twenty years.

In addition to time spent in her office, Willis actively sells herself and her concern throughout the country. Perhaps her early exposure in Hawaii impressed her with the commercial value of public relations. Willis articles have appeared, for example, in the *National Observer, Signature, House & Home, Ms.*, as well as in local newspapers. She is involved with the San Francisco Beautiful group and the Multiple Sclerosis Society. A group of Chinese citizens held a meeting discussing San Francisco Chinatown's deterioration; an Oriental friend of Willis's—who respects her knowledge and sentiments—requested her presence. A delegate to Habitat—the U.N. Conference on Human Settlements—representing the American Institute of Architects and the National Academy of Sciences, Willis is writing a book on condominiums. She is also on the board considering creating a construction museum in the old Pension Building in Washington, D.C., as well as on the Building Researchers' Advisory Board of the National Academy of Sciences and the chairman of the Federal Construction Council. Willis, an award-winner for her renovation of a San Francisco Victorian area, lectures at colleges and to groups concerned about architecture design and the environment.

An inquisitive individual, when Willis wants information, she says so, and manages to get it. After several hours of conversation with an interviewer, the likable Willis turns and says, "Now tell me about *your* life." The interviewer does. And Beverly Ann Willis listens brilliantly.

9

INDIAN INGENUITY

Agnes Howard

----••◆••----

AGNES HODGKINSON HOWARD owns the largest individually run ranch on South Dakota's Standing Rock Indian Reservation. Born and raised in North Dakota, this woman, in her middle sixties—warm, smiling, feminine—is of Sioux Indian extraction. And she credits her native American ancestry in part for her success: "They're always putting Indians down. I have no problems with it. Being Indian. They think I maybe can't do it. Well, I can do it just as good and maybe a little better.... When I do something, I do it with all my heart. To show 'em I can do it... You can do anything if you want to do it bad enough.... They say you can't do anything with nothing. Well, I beg to differ. I think you can. You can always make something do until you get something better. I really believe that." Born in 1912 to an American Indian-German mother and a British father, Agnes Hodgkinson Howard is legally a Sioux Indian. At the time of her birth, the government was having difficulty locating homesteaders for the vast reservation lands of the West. A program was instituted where each child registered with the tribe as an Indian would receive a parcel of land at birth; Agnes became the owner of 160 acres near the Grand River in north-central South Dakota.

Agnes's slight Western speech inflections suggest a quiet strength as her tan face creases with smile lines; she speaks softly, slowly, never wasting words, as she remembers her childhood. Her father, Edward Hodgkinson, traveled from England to what he considered the land of opportunity, and lived in Pennsylvania, eventually settling in North Dakota because he wanted to see the "Wild West."

A sign painter by trade—his daughter says, "He done fancy work. He was sort of an artist"—he tried ranching after marrying an eighteen-year-old Sioux-German girl, Annie Menz. Annie, who had straight black hair and seductive dark eyes, settled with her thirty-five-year-old husband along the Cedar River to develop a ranch.

Through the years, the Hodgkinsons managed to increase their few cattle to a thousand head, but, according to his daughter Agnes, her father tried feed-farming somewhat ahead of his time. "He had a great big steam tractor and that thing cost a hundred dollars a day to run. . . . He went a little too fast." His venture into farming could not be supported by his cattle business long enough to become profitable. So Edward Hodgkinson turned back to ranching and, says his daughter, "He got pretty well on his feet again until he retired."

Agnes Hodgkinson, who was the seventh child in her family of six girls and three boys, remembers, "We all worked hard"—housekeeping, fieldwork, cow-milking. Her face lights up as she recalls her childhood, and her parents. "One of my sisters and I used to milk twenty-one cows before we ever went to school"; they walked a mile to the schoolhouse. In their big family, chores had to be completed. "We were taught that. 'Get your work done first and then there's time for play.'" To polish the wooden flooring in their ten-room farmhouse, she says, her mother "would take this paraffin wax . . . shave it after we got through scrubbing the floors, and we would wrap wool socks around our feet, and then she would turn us loose in there. 'O.K. shine that floor!'. . . . We had a wonderful life, we really did." She smiles and adds, "I guess we were kinda' ornery to the hired hands. . . . We was always playing tricks. We'd put snakes and toads in their beds. . . ." And laughs at the memory.

Her mother attended an Indian school, and Agnes Howard is amazed at the information and knowledge this woman had. "I've often wondered, Where did she learn so much?" She was a peppy vivacious individual who "kept her figure after all her babies." Her daughter adds, "But my father was the head of the family." Her parents had an understanding: "They didn't baby us. . . . Everything Dad said, went." As a child, she thought they were too strict, she says, "and then when I grew up I realized how lucky I was that they instilled high qualities in me." She believes Hodgkinson was a knowledgeable, practical person, and her mother sensible. When the children were ill, "they'd take care of us and they'd *always* know what to do. . . . They had a lot of common sense. . . . They had just good common sense." Old portrait photographs show Edward Hodgkinson wearing a mustache and a stern British-aristocrat expression, and his wife staring straight ahead, giving the impression she missed little.

When she was a child, Agnes could speak German. Her mother's father—born in Germany and traveling to the old country every year—wrote letters in German, and, "my mother would read them to us." But, says Agnes, "I could never learn Indian," although she understood it.

Her grandmother was a full-blooded Indian—"probably wore the blanket and the works"—yet Agnes Hodgkinson learned during her school years that she was not immediately identifiable as having Indian blood: "There was a time when the Indians couldn't buy liquor. . . . The high-school guys would all want to drink and they couldn't get it. So they'd make me go in and buy it. When I was younger. And had dark hair. . . . I was never turned away." She says people thought she was Greek or Jewish. (Today she has a beautiful head of thick silver hair, cut short.)

Before entering secondary school, she attended a girls' Indian school in Bismarck, the capital of North Dakota, yet still a small city. After a year, she traveled home to Thunderhawk High School.

"I always had good marks in school." Active in the glee club, girls' basketball, and cheerleading, "it was something to do" in quiet North Dakota. "We never had swimming pools or stuff like that." They swam in rivers.

She did not date in high school: "Dad was too strict." The Hodgkinson girls attended get-togethers but were not allowed to go alone. There were boys she cared for in high school. And fathers can't control hearts—"you bet they can't." She remembers his finding her romantic letters and notes and tearing them up. "He was real strict with us girls, and we used to say, 'Dad, how come the boys can go and we can't?'" He would then give them some straight facts on why it was all right for his sons and not his daughters. He was an outspoken man. "Oh, you bet!"—a favorite expletive of hers.

As she and her sisters and brothers left home for careers or marriage, her intention to hold on to the acreage she received at birth was strong. One of the benefits of being an Indian—and she indicates there is prejudice, but does not dwell upon it—was the land she was allotted, and still owns. This is unusual. Her brothers and sisters also received property but sold it, often for only two or three dollars an acre. They were not interested in—nor could they foresee the possibility of—being financially able to utilize the land. She is now the only member of her large family to live on a ranch. "Most of my sisters became housewives and mothers," in cities.

After high school, Agnes moved to Oklahoma and enrolled in a business course at the Ponca City Business College while living with a sister. She began dating—"I did. You bet!"—boating, golfing, and attending dances, although "I never got too involved with anyone."

Completing her business-school studies, she worked in several capacities in Oklahoma: comptometer operator, retail cashier, office worker. But she continued to feel she wanted to spend her life on a ranch. "Somehow in the spring of the year, it killed me to just sit in the office. I just wanted to be out in the country."

Her desire to be a rancher was strong when she met her spouse-to-be, J. Dan Howard. "I never got married until I was twenty-eight years old." Howard was a good-looking man. "I thought he was. In my estimation he was." J. Dan, who was five feet ten inches tall, was a gentle individual. "Oh, once in a while we had our little spats like everyone else, but he was fairly easy to get along with." Agnes Hodgkinson Howard adds that her husband was "more Indian than me"; he was concerned with Indian problems and rights as he earned money as a painter, like her father, until World War II began. J. Dan Howard immediately joined the Navy.

When he enlisted, his bride said to herself, "Well, I'm not going to sit around here and twiddle my thumbs." Agnes's mother had recently died, so she took her youngest sister, just graduated from high school, "under my wing," and together they shared an apartment and found work in Oklahoma. Married for one year, she applied for a position the day before her husband left and started working the day after. "I couldn't sit still. I couldn't just sit home. There was nothing for me to sit home for. No children."

During the three years her husband was away, she saw him three times. A Seabee, he spent the duration of the war in Trinidad. She missed him. "At first, it was kind of tough but you get used to it. You know, when you are involved in things, that helps." She and her sister moved to Wichita, and they worked several evenings each week as volunteers in a local hospital or knitting for the Red Cross. "I could never get the mittens done but I made a lot of scarves." Agnes Howard smiles her soft smile. "I was never tempted to be unfaithful," she states, looking astonished at the question, "but you know, I kind of thought that was a sin." She remembers noticing attractive males: "It's just natural that you do. . . . It is hard." But told herself to "toe the mark."

After spending about a year in Kansas, she traveled to North Dakota to work for a federal soil-conservation agency while applying for an appointment with the Bureau of Indian Affairs, a civil-service position. With the soil-conservation group she learned about farming, acreage analysis, ranching, and ranch-financing, and her dream to own her own ranch became more persistent. About the time her husband returned, she obtained her long-hoped-for job at the Bureau of Indian Affairs; he again worked as a painter. "And I kept talking to him about cattle."

Owing to his Indian ancestry, J. Dan Howard had received his 160 acres at birth, as his wife had. Agnes repeats, "I'm the only one in my family that still has my original lot," including her husband. After their marriage he sold his stake—she was against it—and bought a car with the proceeds: "He wanted to sell it; I couldn't stop him. . . . I didn't think it was a good idea. I wanted him to keep it but he didn't agree. So I said, 'If that's the way you feel about it, you can sell yours. I'm not going to sell my land.'" The car was the Howards' first automobile.

Agnes Howard continued discussing cattle-ranching with her husband. With her encouragement, he bought books on agriculture, and after years of trying to convince him—"We could put together a unit. There's all this land. Let's get a loan and start out"—he finally agreed.

It was almost impossible for an Indian to borrow funds from regular sources—the Farmers' Home Administration or other government programs. "So," Agnes says, "we got a loan from the tribe," at 4½ percent, from a fund designed to help fellow Indians wishing to start businesses.

Her land—on the Standing Rock Reservation in Sioux County, South Dakota—was combined with four leased sections of unimproved range containing no buildings, fences, or wells. The only water available was from the Grand River and was used for their cattle, which they obtained through the reservation cattle pool.

Agnes Howard did not wish to farm. "Strictly cattle," she says. They purchased twenty-eight head and built a small two-room house while Agnes continued working for the Bureau of Indian Affairs to support the ranch.

"Every Friday after work, I'd be all packed and ready." She commuted a hundred miles to the Howard Ranch to spend weekends with her husband. "I'd bake bread, cookies . . . and late on Sunday afternoon I'd go back." When asked about the years of separation, she quips, "Had less fights!" Then she adds playfully, "I used to like to have a fight with him," because she enjoyed the "making up." The couple lived on twenty dollars a week after ranch-related expenses.

The Howard enterprise began in 1952; in 1964 they installed indoor plumbing. "My operation was rather crude to start with," she says. The first corrals were made from timber collected while clearing the land.

Her interest was in ranching, but although she managed to

convince her husband to try it, he was never fully involved. "I think one of the biggest fights we ever had was when I figured he should pay more attention to our enterprise rather than get involved in politics."

J. Dan Howard disagreed. He became more deeply immersed in the political side of Indian affairs. "You know, you can't be two or three places and do justice to it. . . . I felt he was neglecting our enterprise, especially when I'd be commuting." An acquaintance of J. Dan Howard's said, "I wouldn't say he didn't like to work cattle. . . . But he felt the obligation to represent his people more strongly. He got so involved he didn't have a whole lot of time. . . ." Agnes Howard quit work, moved across the state line to South Dakota, and ran the ranch.

During the years the ranch was being developed, teen-age boys worked for the Howards during the summer, living in the bunkhouse. "And then they'd come over here for meals. I'd cook for them," comments Agnes Howard. She and her spouse had no children themselves: "My husband was burned years ago. His mother used a big pot of water to do her wash in, and he was trying to learn his little sister how to walk. And he was walking backwards. And his mother had set the pot on the floor and he fell in. . . . That made him sterile." In addition to the summer boys, she became a den mother and a Girl Scout leader; her husband was involved with junior league baseball when he was home.

But often he traveled, frequently to Congressional hearings in Washington. Through her husband she met nationally known politicians, which she enjoyed. But she repeats, "I didn't care too much for my husband being so involved. There were times . . . when he got snowbound. I remember once when a three-day storm hit when we were starting to calve. . . . I had the calves on my kitchen floor!" Every time a baby calf—the link to the successfully run ranch—died, she would think, There goes a hundred-dollar bill.

The Howards hired a man to help with work she could not do alone. The ranch grew in size under her overseeing as J. Dan Howard became Tribal Chairman, the equivalent to Chief. And although she today continues to feel he should have spent more time on the ranch, she does admit, "Someone had to do what he did" for the Indian cause.

The creation of the Howard Ranch was the result of the original land allotment to Agnes Howard at birth, financial assistance from the tribe, and a tribal revolving livestock loan of twenty-eight head. The cattle were repaid with the Herefords the Howard cows produced over the years rather than with cash.

In 1955, the Howards were able to settle their loans completely. Mrs. Howard decided it was time to add to her herd; one cannot make money with twenty-eight head. By 1960 she owned over a hundred cattle and had added about eight hundred acres to the four leased sections.

In the late sixties, while Ag—as her friends call her—was running her ranch, J. Dan was hospitalized in Washington. "He was ill and had a stroke, but this business—politics—meant so much to him that he just kept pushing himself." When he became sick again and was in the Bismarck hospital, a two-hour drive from the ranch, his wife planned to get an apartment to stay with him. He commented, "Hell, no, you'd better get home and run that ranch." She stayed in North Dakota a week and returned to the Howard Ranch "to get the boys to hay." And when her husband died she continued, in his words, to "run that ranch."

At his death, according to a friend, he was "still a young-looking, good-looking guy. . . . I think Ag kinda blocks it out now. I think it took her a while. . . ." For a period of time, she was taken advantage of. One helping neighbor, according to her present foreman, "took quite a few of her calves. . . ." In addition, she was "plagued with bad health." But she managed? "Oh, *yeah.*"

Ag Howard says she's had a good life. She does not consider remarriage: "I'm free this way. I don't have to cook for someone, I don't have to wash clothes for anyone. I feel free and I'm getting used to being alone. And at least I can stand myself. And I love people. And I like the way I live. And I have freedom." But what about a man's companionship? Do you miss that? "I did at first, but I don't any more."

After her husband's death, she continued to develop her business, adding to her native grass by planting 158 acres of alfalfa, then building a barn, erecting corrals, repairing and replacing fencing. A new bunkhouse and three new stock wells were added. She hired men to put up hay, aid at calving time, and generally help manage the ranchland.

Her life revolves around her ranch, presently about 40,000 acres. "I'm expanding all the time. . . ." Casually and with authority she discusses overgrazing and rotating. At the time of J. Dan Howard's death, Agnes Howard decided it was prudent to discontinue her crossbreeding program, and converted to a strictly Hereford cattle program, doubling her herd.

The reservation includes over two hundred thousand acres of land still held by the tribe. Before 1919, there were few Indians who wanted to live on the reservation land, and those who did were scattered along the rivers. The Howard Ranch foreman, Jim Gilland, an Indian, explains, "They wanted to live together. They didn't want to spread out." Gilland adds that the government "opened it up to homesteading in 1909 . . . and that really checkerboarded the reservation." About half of the land in the reservation is now privately owned, by Indians and others. Today his boss can lease tribal-owned Indian land—she has first preference—before a non-Indian can. "It *is* Indian land," she comments.

Gilland says some of Howard's neighbors are envious of her priority: "They'd like to have it themselves. They'd like nothing better than for me and her to not get along [so the ranch would fold]. They're white people. They can't lease." Gilland says there is prejudice against these people though they are not visually identifiable as Indians. "There is. I felt that all my life." He adds, almost inaudibly, that no one tries to hide the fact they are of Indian extraction.

Jim Gilland, with a quiet country voice interspersed with silent pauses, is in his thirties. His family has known Ag Howard for years. As the Agnes Howard Ranch foreman and overseer of his three brothers, who work on the ranch, he says his boss is an individualist and he finds her a feminine woman. Out of her earshot he comments softly, "She would be attractive to me if she was in my age group," and says his fiancée reminds him of Ag in many ways. "She's got a mind of her own, too." (Agnes Howard comments, when her foreman is not present, "You know, I wish he was my age or I was his age.") Howard relies on Gilland to take care of things for her. When she's old and feeble? "I'm not ever going to get feeble." She laughs, and adds, "I'm taking him under my wing. He's a good cowman. I've known him all my life. He's a *heck* of a nice guy." She clicks her tongue as she speaks.

His silence almost masking his intelligence, Jim Gilland drives his boss's pickup truck—with a package of Copenhagen snuff on the dashboard—across the Howard land. Past the tin-roof barn with the birds flying inside as a grazing horse stares. It is another beautiful day in South Dakota where clouds are rare and the unpolluted sky is clear blue. The air smells clean. Driving to a ridge overlooking the flat glacially scoured landscape, one sees in the distance, near a pile of several bales of hay, the Howard

Hereford cattle grazing. A muddy trail winds across land too sloppy for a truck after recent rains. The rolling topography, with trees in the distance, is interrupted by small plateaus in the shadows. Gumbo banks—a type of soil that develops over shale-rock outcroppings, which gets slick when it is wet and where nothing will grow—drops down to the hundred-foot-wide Grand River, feeding into the Missouri. The Standing Rock Reservation countryside is desolate. One drives for tens of miles without passing a car. "There's a lot of country out here," Howard comments. The hills of South Dakota are dotted with large rocks—erratics—dropped by glaciers twelve thousand or more years ago, and as the sun shines on them they appear purple and ominous. ("I bet there could be a lot of snakes up there, too," she says casually. Her niece comments, "I've seen her kill a snake.")

Howard says, "In ought-six there was a cyclone" in the depression behind her house. Previously her land was an Army camp, then a Sioux settlement, and finally an Indian missionary area. Chief Thunderhawk, buried on her land, camped there with his followers when Sitting Bull was killed about a hundred miles away. She purchased this additional acreage, not part of her inherited property, from Chief Thunderhawk's heirs.

On the quarter-mile between the Grand River and her home is a stand of box elders and cottonwoods. Wild grapes and wild plums give her a chance to do something else a ranchwoman does: Howard cans juices and jellies. Gilland says Agnes Howard is a fine cook. "Real good. Yeah." He says "yeah" much like a Vermonter. "About anything she tries to cook is good." In the latter part of May at roundup time, as cowboys are vaccinating, castrating, dehorning, and branding, the five-foot-three-inch woman in her sixties makes a roast for about twenty-five workers and serves it on the range. She puts a thick slab of Howard meat on a huge roll, with beans and potato salad.

She refers to her workers as "the boys" and enjoys their company during daylight hours. In the evening she is alone in her tiny home. At the time of her husband's death there were plans to build a new house. Afterward she decided to leave things as they were. J. Dan Howard's hat still hangs on a hook in the kitchen. Other than that, there are no reminders. No photographs. Agnes Howard believes in looking ahead.

Jim Gilland says, "Ag knows what she wants to do and sets her mind to it and does it. She doesn't rely on someone else to make her decisions. She'll talk things over, but she pretty much makes up her own mind." She is definitely in charge, yet never actually orders anyone around. She lets him know when she's dissatisfied: " 'I'm mad'—that's all she says."

Acquaintances say Ag Howard's English heritage is apparent; they seem to be saying the woman has class. "Right . . . that's exactly what it is. She just *has* it." It's that same special something the self-made woman in Hombly Hills, Chicago, or New York possesses. Sophistication? No. Not in the middle of the Dakotas in an unpretentious home among simple people. What she has—in common with other special females—is that self-assured carriage, awareness of her own ability, brains, and drive, and womanliness. A relative says, "She can go out, mend a fence, and still be totally feminine."

Howard's foreman remembers her joining the workers at roundup time for years, but now, he says, "She'll help but she doesn't do as much." But she is active. With roosters, turkeys, and geese making their individual sounds, Howard wakes early after six hours of sleep, stretches, and says, with her closed-lip smile, "It's so quiet out here you wouldn't believe it. I slept good. As usual"—at an age when many women complain of insomnia. She slips a pair of snug-fitting jeans over her still-fine figure, with a sweater that accentuates her full bust. She weighs the same in her

Agnes Howard, Rancher

sixties as she did when she was a teen. A collector of turquoise jewelry, she slips on a squash-blossom necklace and two rings.

As she enters her kitchen, the intercom connecting to the bunkhouse crackles. The cowboys have a problem. Putting on her leather jacket and old worn leather gloves, she goes to look over the situation. Gilland: "She knows cattle real well. She recognizes and knows each of her individual cows." Howard discusses her stock: "I culled real deep and bought back. I sold a hundred head of cattle and I bought back a hundred head. And they were the Black cows." She smiles. "If one cow is missing, I know it." Her knowledge of ranching is well known and respected. In a 1976 *Dakota Farmer* issue, she was featured in the article "Women in Dakota Agriculture." She is a committee-woman on the Farmers' Home Administration and secretary-treasurer of the Standing Rock Cattlemen's Association. "She's part of everything," says her niece.

"I have no complaints." And she grins a Mona Lisa smile as she goes to turn the chickens out and feed them. According to her foreman, Ag Howard treats her chickens like babies. Her comment: "I love to watch those chickens grow. It's a good feeling. They give me something to worry about, something to care for." She laughs her soft laugh.

Gilland: "I'm a little disgusted with her for getting so many chickens. I didn't think she needed *that* many chickens. ["Chickens" is said with disdain.] She was supposed to get one hundred but she came back with four hundred!" He laments the small size of the chicken coop. "She can change her mind quick like that sometimes. She makes snap decisions on her own. I think if I'd been there I'd of talked about how much room we've got." She admits the Howard Ranch chicken population *is* a bit high. Gilland softens. "She'll be butchering them off pretty soon."

Howard's twenty-year-old horse, Kemo, watches her from his

pasture beyond the coop. The quarter-horse—ridden too hard by a hand—is now lame. James Gilland is peeved with Howard's reluctance to get rid of her old worn-out horse: "I kinda see it, though. She's had him most of his life—so long she's attached to him."

Agnes Howard is fond of her cockapoo Ringo as well. An erratic canine, he is consistently affectionate and protective of his mistress, who rarely leaves him behind when traveling in the Dakotas.

Local trips take hours because of the vast distances between towns. When Agnes Howard is ready (she is always prompt), she walks to her car, which might have duck droppings on the hood and a turkey on the roof. In wintertime, Hershey bars, warm clothing, and a sleeping bag are stowed in the auto in case of a breakdown on the desolate roads. Her foreman says she is a fine driver. Cautious. There is a bull horn installed in her new Pontiac, as well as a C.B. radio, not for entertainment but as a method of communication when lines are down.

A gravel truck road leads from her home past her mailbox three miles away, then twenty-two miles north to the "one-horse town," as she says, of Morristown, South Dakota. Service station, general store, town hall, community building, post office. "This is one of my banks." She points. Bar and grill, two churches.

While shopping in the general store, she speaks to men concerning the repair of her tornado-damaged bunkhouse. "We'll have to sit down and do some estimating," she says. "Yes, ma'am, Mrs. Howard," one answers. She is not sure when "the boys"—her cowhands—can help with the repair. "This month we're doing hayfields; next month coming we're going to be selling calves. It's going to take us a week to round up because we're selling five hundred head of calves out there."

Back on the roads, paralleling monotonous electrical wire poles along one side. Past fields of wheat, oats, corn, some barley, sunflowers; it's a two-hour drive to Bismarck. One of her hands says, "She likes to go shopping and do other things women like to do." Fastidiously, Agnes Howard washes new-clothing purchases before wearing them.

Howard tries on several outfits when she is going out. According to her niece, "No matter what the occasion, she will take an extra change in the car." She might be halfway to a restaurant and decide she should have worn the eighth outfit she tried on instead of the tenth. "I'll travel one hundred miles for a good meal," Howard states but in the next breath she says restaurant food is expensive. Usually she stays home.

Cooking, relaxing, or talking business, she is usually in the most frequented room in the Howard home, the kitchen, where cattle prices are reported over the radio. She may light another Marlboro and smile when she is asked a question. If a rhetorical statement is made, she does not murmur agreement but remains silent. When an answer is not absolutely necessary, she'll not give it. At the same time, she is not reticent about voicing an opinion, which she offers in her soft, low, pleasant voice.

Enjoyment for this unassuming attractive woman includes visiting her family once a year. "I try to see all my sisters." Does she wish she had children? "In this day and age, I don't know." And adds, "It would be nice in my old age to have children." She has a close relationship with her niece Phyllis—in her early thirties—who visits Howard when in need of emotional strength: "Ag just whips me back into shape. You don't think negative around her; you think positive."

"I'm getting to the age where I'm taking all the short cuts I can. . . . I do what I want to do and when I want to do it," declares Howard, who enjoys fishing and dreams of having a catfish farm on her land. With a fish shack down by her river, she'll sit by the Grand with her rod and reel all day. "She loves it," a relative comments. In the fall, she fly-casts for trout in the Montana mountains. "I can handle worms or frogs or whatever. It doesn't make any difference to me. If you can't bait your own hook, you have no business fishing." She often catches northern pike, walleyes. Her beautifully golden-tanned yet soft skin indicates she spends time in the sun. "I've been chopping wood," she says as she walks past the cowboy boots lined up in the entranceway to look over her land, explaining that she had no one to guide her toward her goal: "I just done a lot of reading. Being how I had been born and raised on a ranch, it just came natural for me. It was *in* me. It was in my blood and it came so easily for me. . . . It is my life. I continued to operate after my husband died, and I'll continue as long as I can walk." On the basis of her intelligent common sense, energy, and enthusiasm, she'll be in business for a long time. When asked if J. Dan Howard was as peppy as his widow, her niece commented, "Do you think *anyone* is as peppy as she is?" Ag Howard's niece shakes her head. "I've never seen anyone who has taken the gift of life and made something of it as she has."

Jim Gilland on Howard: "Ag isn't hard for anyone to get along with. Just treat her fair. It does get her dander up when someone pulls a dirty deal. . . . I respect her a lot for that. She'll say what she thinks." He adds that mentally she's probably as bright as any man. When asked if she is sharper than some, the foreman stops, considers, and sidesteps. "She's on the ball."

Agnes Howard, the rancher, does everything a woman is supposed to do, and all a man does as well. She disagrees: "Not *everything* a man does. I don't compare myself to a man. But I'm not afraid to do anything."

10

RIGHT SMART

Barbara Gardner Proctor

———————◆———————

THE SCENE is a Chicago top-line business club, and the group—
the Illinois State Chamber of Commerce—is made up of state
bankers, industry presidents, and wives. And Barbara Proctor. On
the board of directors of the Chamber, Mrs. Proctor is escorted,
as usual, by her business and personal associate, George Miller.

Each member of this élite group in heartland America rises, in
turn, to introduce himself and his spouse. It becomes Miller's
and Proctor's turn: she takes the initiative, stands erect, and
states: "I am Barbara Proctor, of Proctor & Gardner Advertising,
and"—she points to her companion—"this is my wife, George
Miller." The roomful of wall-to-wall WASP Illinoisians doubles
up with laughter.

The solid Midwestern gentlemen enjoy having Proctor—a
black female—create the aura of liberalism around them and
their organization. This woman—who has been heard to state, "I
can't be bothered with your prejudices. That's your problem"—
shines among the men and their wives as a touch of charm, style,

and poise. Later, over liqueurs, the bankers comment among themselves that Barbara is on their board because she is competent and intelligent, not because she is a black or a woman. These men are interested in speaking to Barbara, pipeline to the ills of the ghettos, a respectable source of information who knows which fork to use and how to speak softly and with dignity—totally acceptable at a sophisticated business gathering.

"I think white people are sincere," comments Proctor's executive secretary, Lanoitte McLurkin: "The fact that she is black and she is the way she is—so outgoing, so positive—they get caught up in it, too. And I think the color stops right there. They want to help her. They see her as a human being, not a black, not a woman. And at the bottom line the fact that she is black makes them want to do it more. Her color is a plus in her case. And on top of that she is a woman, too."

George Miller—white—on Proctor: "White people are very anxious to know Barbara Proctor. . . . If you are trying to put together a hoitsy-toitsy cocktail party, it's chic to have a well-known black."

In a social setting, Proctor announces she's from the wrong side of the hill in Black Mountain, North Carolina, and employee George Miller is a private-school WASP, "from the word go." She adds, "Between the two of us, we can cover the waterfront."

Proctor is the high point at many gatherings. At the Chamber of Commerce dinner the men, who refer to her as colored rather than black, sit over dinner talking national politics, as they listen to her comments. One says, "Tell me, Barbara, how did you get your start? Wasn't your husband involved in the business with you?" She hides an amused smirk. "No," she says. "I am Gardner and I am Proctor." (She confidently gives her analysis of Proctor at work/play at such a social gathering: "I am working throughout the whole thing . . . when things are going to lull, when someone's wife is feeling unattended, when a husband has had too much to drink. You've got to keep it all working. It's serious; it's really hard work." The diplomatic corps could use Proctor.)

Always the businesswoman–advertising executive, Proctor is filling ears with public relations related to one of her accounts, a large urban residential package with zoning problems. These influential men might be useful to her.

Of the Chamber of Commerce members, she says, "They're fun people . . . they think I'm so weird. . . . I have the greatest time among them because they just think I'm the strangest person they have ever met in their entire lives. I think one evening of me gives them conversation for six months!" She laughs her deep-throated laugh.

At all times during the occasion, she is selling herself. She *is* Proctor & Gardner, epitomizing the advertising-agency style, the image, the creativeness, and the ability to get things done.

The liquor flows and so does Proctor, totally self-assured as the only black in the room and the only woman director, as she walks from man to man in her elegant three-quarter-length black tuxedo coat, white ruffled low-cut silk blouse, and long black A-line skirt. Her determined chin juts slightly as she makes a point, her eyes shining with enthusiasm and challenge.

She slipped into her elegant tux at work after a day which included Kraft Foods' acceptance of the three-million-dollar Proctor & Gardner presentation. Carefully combing her soft straight head of black wig hair, applying makeup to caramel-colored lids, she listened to the evening news with one ear and at the same time chatted with business associates. Then her secretary handed her a typed index card listing where Proctor was going for the evening, what time she was to arrive, and driving directions for

Miller. (She never remembers how to get places.) Everything is smooth-running, well organized.

The room where she changes—she calls it her president's office, as opposed to another room, her creative office—is elegant. Mirrored walls, modernistic lamps, foiled wallpaper, plush carpeting, and a catty-cornered desk with lucite accessories give the room an upbeat stylish ad-agency look. It is an apartment setting created within her business complex. The TV in the corner is on, constantly tuned to Chicago's Channel 2, one of her clients. Other past and present accounts include Jewel, Gallo Winery, Gillette, Paper Mate, Sears.

Barbara Gardner Proctor did not start life in such surroundings. Her father, William Gardner, and her mother, Bernice Baxter, were unmarried in 1932 when Barbara was born, and nonetheless surnamed Gardner. After her child's birth, sixteen-year-old Bernice Baxter enrolled in secretarial school, leaving her baby in a woman's care: "My grandmother—I come from a long line of very strong women—had split up with her husband, and my mother [one of seven children] was one of the older ones at fourteen. The older girls went out to find jobs. . . . I was four years old before my grandmother knew I was on the face of the earth, because my mother had boarded me with a family in Ashville . . . till my grandmother found out there was a 'me.' And she sent for me and I grew up with her. . . ." The child never lived with her mother—"I embarrass her by saying I'm illegitimate"—who moved to Washington, D.C., worked at the newly built Pentagon, where she's still employed, married, and sent money home to help support her child. "But she never shared herself," states her daughter. "She just never liked to share herself a lot."

There was no man in Barbara's grandmother's house. Barbara's mother's brothers—her uncles—were in their late teens and early twenties, and began going to war. "I grew up . . . without a male presence in the home all my life. . . . It has never occurred to me to look for Daddy to do something."

Proctor says her religious, proud grandmother was "a super lady, with a grace about her. I thought she was just the most beautiful thing in the world"—a heavyset woman with "gorgeous streaked hair."

The family lived in a shack, "dirt-poor," with no water, no electricity. Barbara's grandmother, Coralee Baxter, worked as a cook at a local college and in the summer as a maid: "She worked very hard. If there ever was a guiding force in my life it was my grandmother. . . . She was loving, she was affectionate; beyond that she was extremely strong and reputable. She had a great deal of dignity, had a sense of reality. She is the one who taught me to accept whatever your circumstances are, but first admit that *is* the circumstance. Because it is only when you admit that, that you can deal with it." In summertime the white people from far south came to North Carolina for vacations. Coralee Baxter cleaned and readied their cottages. For this work she received two dollars a day, and, Proctor remembers, "I would get a quarter if I went along. And I would go with her to clean those houses and sometimes these nice little Southern belles would come up there [and notice Barbara] and say [her voice becomes Southern and dramatic and condescending], 'God, Coralee, that sure is a cute little thing.' And my grandmother would look at me and say, 'Oh, no. She's not cute but she's right smart. And she's going to amount to something someday.' And I was about five or six and ugly as sin. And she said, 'Not cute but right smart.'"

Her grandmother convinced her on both counts. Barbara excelled in school and insists she was ugly: "Seriously. A bad-news kid. And it occurred to me . . . that I could get friends if I could do their homework. And so that meant that I had to study everything. . . . You have to trade with your mind, your personality, or you have to develop something that will stay with you long after your beauty is gone. It's not a bad deal. It's not a complaint when I say I was an ugly kid. I *was* an ugly kid . . . but it never stopped me from doing anything. I still got what I wanted." A cheerleader and drummer in the band, she worked on the school paper and yearbook. "Skinny as a rail." Her deep loud laughter bubbles out. "I didn't have much going for me."

When she graduated from high school, she planned to marry Johnny Welles. As she speaks of this long-ago romance, her voice—always crisp and clear—becomes deeper, agreeably husky, and she enunciates for emphasis, her eyes wide and bright. Welles looked like a black John Wayne, a tall, gorgeous man. "That's all I wanted to do. Marry Johnny and live happily ever after." But it didn't happen.

Barbara's mother "swooped down from Washington to Black Mountain to knock some sense into me." Bernice Baxter Alexander filed applications for her daughter with three colleges; all accepted the excellent student. But Barbara was adamant; she was going to marry Johnny, not attend school.

Welles himself ended it. He decided he didn't "want me dumb. He not only stopped seeing me, he started dating my best friend!" That was not very nice. "No, it was *very* nice . . . because I'm basically a very reticent person about leaving a situation I enjoy." Today Johnny Welles is a blue-collar worker with eight children, "working in a factory somewhere. I haven't kept track of him the last five or six years." She never saw him again.

She went to Talladega College in Alabama—"heartbroken, wounded all the way"—majored and minored in education and English and graduated in three years, then stayed an extra year for an additional major and minor in psychology and sociology. Along with a scholarship, Barbara received help from her mother and worked herself.

After college, which included friendships with men but no romantic involvements, she obtained a job at the Circle Pine Camp in Kalamazoo, Michigan. On her way home at summer's end, she stopped in Chicago and spent her total camp earnings, including carfare home. "I'm still prone to do crazy things like that. . . . I'm still looking for my carfare," she joshes.

Her last fling was at a beauty salon; a friendly beautician took her in until she earned enough to rent a one-room furnished apartment. Evenings she listened and fell in love with the voice of a disk jockey, Sidney McCoy. "He had the most magnificent voice in the world—it was so sexy—and I listened from twelve midnight till four in the morning." It became an obsession. "This was just the most magnificent person since Johnny." Remembering her old tack that trading on "beauty and the bod" doesn't work, she went to the record shop McCoy owned, but rarely frequented, and volunteered to inventory about ten thousand records. So after finishing her regular daytime job at five o'clock she went to McCoy's store and worked till ten o'clock. "Then I listened to him," she says, until four in the morning.

It took three weeks to meet him, and eventually his wife and children. The McCoys and Barbara became friends and the disk jockey—also an employee of Vee-Jay Records—obtained a position for her with Vee-Jay, writing descriptive comments on album backs.

McCoy was a jazz expert. His friendship and her position with Vee-Jay Records eventually enabled Barbara to meet artists such as Cannonball Adderley, Nancy Wilson, Ray Charles, Miles Davis, John Coltrain. She decided to free-lance jazz feature-writing and submitted a piece to *Downbeat* magazine which was accepted.

When *Downbeat* was looking for a full-time jazz writer, they approached her. "So I developed that whole thing of living in the jazz world at night. . . ." In time, she became Vee-Jay's international director at $17,000 a year, with a company car, an apartment, and an expense account.

In the late fifties, she attended the Newport Jazz Festival as a jazz writer and met Sarah Vaughan's ("Sarah was a friend of mine") road manager, Carl Proctor, and "the upshot of that is the fifth time I ever saw him I got married. It sounds too tacky to be true... but I really got married because I got bored—nothing else to do." A "life-of-the-party type," of West Indian descent, Carl Proctor had a "fiery, exciting kind of" personality.

Married in July, she was pregnant by December: "I was also bored with marriage." It was difficult for her to be accountable to anyone; she misses a single person's flexibility, while he—a road person—enjoyed the stability of married life.

By this time, Barbara Gardner had become a well-known international jazz critic. People recognized her and her name; they didn't know Carl Proctor. "So we had that problem." Several times he was called Mr. Gardner. (Barbara continued to use her maiden name.) They separated on their second wedding anniversary, she says, "basically because I felt it was respectable to stay married two years." His resentful feelings made it difficult to continue to share the jazz profession. She quit her job.

Barbara Gardner Proctor then entered what she calls "the twilight time of my life." It was 1962, she was thirty-one years old, and "it was monstrous." She sees this period as a crisis time for women—and for her. After a marvelous life-style, she began to "literally live off of secretaries—friends—little people." They helped her as she waited for the right job. "Twenty dollars a week here and thirty dollars a week there."

When the marriage ended, the former jazz critic was leasing a thirteen-room apartment, which she managed to keep although she had no furniture, simply a refrigerator and wall-to-wall carpeting. She stayed in that apartment for five years while doing odd jobs and searching for the right market for her abilities and talents. In 1961, she went to Black Mountain for her grandmother's funeral, then wrote an article around the idea that you *can* go home again. *"Déjà vu.* You see yourself ten years ago." It was published in a "little" magazine, *The Paper.* A book publisher saw her story. For $1,800 she agreed to expand it into a book, but she never revised it. Several temporary jobs and free-lance articles in *Downbeat* brought in more cash.

In 1963—the year Kennedy was killed—some of the advertising agencies decided to hire a black person. "White folk were pretending they wanted to get involved with black folks." She was interviewed by an ad man who, "with all the ignorance of the entire white establishment" [her voice sharpens for emphasis], said he wanted to put a black in an important position. What his agency considered an important job for a black was not the same for a white employee, according to Barbara. Advertising is a team business; the interviewer was not sure how others would work with a black. "Oh, it was so humiliating . . . the most humiliating experience of my life."

Yet the advertising business intrigued her and, applying for another advertising job, she was offered it if she agreed to change her last name, as Gardner was part of the name of the agency. Ironically, Barbara Gardner Proctor, who was not known by her married name while she lived with Carl Proctor, now became Barbara Proctor. She adds that Mr. Gardner, the boss, was not privy to all this. And when he found out he insisted she become Barbara Gardner again. She chose not to.

"I was the first black in advertising in the city of Chicago." From her international jazz critic position, "I went from all my great wonderness . . . to writing the backs of PineSol labels. At eight thousand five hundred a year . . . I learned the whole business from the ground up." A fellow employee, creative director

Gene Taylor, "who more than any other single person in the advertising world is responsible for everything I've done," gave her a variety of responsibilities during the five years. Her mentor? "I would say in advertising, yes."

Barbara Gardner Proctor sits and talks easily in her creative office where a soft-gold sofa winds around the rice-papered room, containing slim black venetian blinds, huge planters, and a square coffee table. A silk-screened design hangs on the wall. Proctor & Gardner's offices are in a new skyscraper located in the modern Illinois Center. She leans back, sips coffee, and remembers her mentor being fired for political reasons. "When he left, I left." At that point she felt she knew the business well.

"And that's when I learned you really don't make decisions . . ." unless you are the boss. She had a set of opinions and a specific kind of experience, and would only take a position where she would not have to "knuckle under. By now," she recalls, "I'm well over thirty"; she couldn't get into a temporary situation, and advertising, she asserts, "is the business of the golden girls . . . under thirty, blond, and all that good stuff. Well, I wasn't *any* of that, so I thought I'd better find something very quickly I could control. . . . When have you ever seen an old ugly advertising woman who did not *own* something?" Either the client or the company. Proctor explains that in the "hot" part of the business "you better be pretty or powerful. Preferably both." Her clear voice becomes distinct and she speaks in a staccato fashion. No one is going to misunderstand Barbara Proctor, whose aliveness, rather than her looks, is predominant.

This woman who says she believes in everything—an illegitimate plain black child from Black Mountain, North Carolina—is respected within her office for her drive. Her energy quickly becomes the subject of any discussion about her. And the way her mind works. According to her vice-president and closest friend, George Miller, "She shoots from the hip."

In 1970, she was shooting for a Small Business Administration loan for $100,000 to begin her own business. Banks responded to the unemployed woman: " 'You're crazy. What is your collateral?' And," she recalls, "I said, 'I am.'" She suggested the bankers check with three diverse advertising agencies for a market value on Barbara Proctor: "I was a *hot* property," having won a number of advertising awards. This was about the time Mary Wells received publicity as she formed her Manhattan agency. An article written about Proctor referred to her as a "black Mary Wells."

Upon asking the worth in dollar-salary per year for Barbara Gardner Proctor, the bankers received three answers: $65,000, said one; $80,000, suggested another; and the third said $110,000. "I got a loan for eighty thousand dollars and I was in business."

But it seems amazing; this was a totally unsecured loan. "Well, *I'm* secure. I'm still here." This was the first service loan guaranteed by the S.B.A. to anyone—male, female, black or white. "They didn't even have the right forms. . . ." Proctor received the original loan. Today they are common.

Proctor & Gardner's creative director Jones remembers: "We started out in small offices at 619 North Wabash. It was an old mansion. Over a pizza place. It was hectic, really hectic." In his pleasant casual voice, he speaks of his woman boss: "She has a lot of self-determination. She's ambitious. She's smart. She's a lot of those things, and she has known what she really wanted to do for some time." Able to organize her life as mother and advertising executive, she is successful "because of her stubbornness," he adds. "She's a very professional person—very demanding. I guess that's my reason for being associated with her for so long, because she does make demands on you . . . and the end result is always good."

"I was in the mailroom when she barely had a typewriter as a junior copywriter," states George Miller, bald-headed, slightly built, vice-president, and escort—the person who, Proctor says, "is probably my closest friend." The likable Miller, product of a WASP upbringing and boarding school, has been called both Mr. Proctor and Mr. Gardner. Miller, single, feels Proctor's success was aided by the fact that she is a woman and a mother, for she is the person many consumer advertisements are directed toward. "Her perspective is very keen."

Miller speaks slowly, perhaps a bit pompously; one waits impatiently for the conclusion of his sentence. In his late thirties, he is the perfect backdrop for Proctor. As he sits quietly by, she bathes

Vice-president George Miller and Barbara Proctor, president, flanked by employees

in the limelight with her glittery gold and diamond jewelry, her chic clothes and her aura of success. Miller explains Barbara Proctor's standards. She wants no clients with a product which negatively stereotypes or adversely affects the black community. While she would take a Lincoln ad, she will not accept as a client Cadillac, a liquor company, or a cigarette firm. A New York City ad executive says she has "a streak of morality," unique in the rat race of advertising. Although Proctor never worked in black advertising before opening her own agency, Proctor & Gardner does, in fact, excel in this particular specialty.

Black and white ad men in three-piece suits are seen scurrying in and out of Proctor & Gardner past the receptionist. The reception area contains a tufted crushed-velvet sofa and thick-piled carpeting, with beige walls, a bust on the cocktail table, and Proctor & Gardner ads hung as artwork. But one's eyes are drawn to the receptionist—a lovely fine-featured black woman—who claims her boss has some kind of E.S.P. "She's sensitive, very sensitive." Starry-eyed, she speaks of her idol, who she feels does not have a male-dominance type of power, rather a faith in herself, a confidence. And that affects people who have contact with her: "Mrs. Proctor always has time to stop and talk on a personal level. . . . She could not pay me enough for me to work as hard as I am. . . . She has her faults . . . *believe me*, but you can take them. If you could bottle her, you could sell her. She runs on a lot of energy."

Dozens of awards hanging on the hallway walls—Achievement in the Business World of Black Women, S.M.I.-Woman's Day Advertising Merit Award, Journal Newspaper Group Creative Award, Dynamic Woman of the Year, Fourth Annual Conference on Business Opportunities for Women Award, Iota Phi Lambda Sorority, "1978 National Headliner by Women in Communications—surround a black, brown, and yellow graphic stripe leading past the conference room, with its movie screen and projection room, toward the glass-walled office of Proctor's executive secretary and personal assistant, Ms. McLurkin.

The secretary has never worked for a woman—"and let me emphasize a *woman*"—so interested in the outside community. "I'm not just going to work, typing all day and collecting a check. I'm actually involved in it with her, and I want to see her succeed." Employees continually express this same personal loyalty to Mrs. Proctor.

Back down the hall to the office of creative director Jones, who is careful with his words: "She doesn't like people overstepping, making decisions without her knowing about it. . . . She's good for most people who work for her. They all get a charge out of her. She has to be driven to really great lengths to yell. . . . I've seen her take so much but she is human, you know? She doesn't harbor grudges. . . . She's basically a creative person. . . . When at work on a creative project, she *never* thinks of the obvious." On the subject of men versus women bosses, he says "Oh, God. Do you have my name in there?" But he laughs softly and acknowledges differences. Men are consistent, the same. They reconsider occasionally and they have their moods. But Jones can, he says, "see where they're coming from. With a woman you really don't know. There is something about women. They will change. They will sometimes second-guess themselves. You do *and do* what you're supposed to do and what you're assigned to do, and she'll have second thoughts and she'll change it." He reluctantly admits that in a creative field it is good to second-guess yourself with totally different ideas. (Proctor on Jones's remarks: "When a male boss changes his mind, he is considered to be showing flexibility, being innovative, and exercising his prerogative. When a woman boss does the same, she's being changeable, irrational, and flighty.") Jones admits it is sometimes trying working for Proctor, "But the end results are always good."

Proctor—who has an almost automatic positive effect on others—should not have to motivate employees, she believes. People must take responsibility for decisions, not look to the boss. They must say to themselves, "I'm going to do it. Sink or swim, I'm going to do it." She will not falsely give credit if, she says, "you've done a dumb-ass thing that has cost me some money," but still expects her workers to "turn around tomorrow and make a new decision." Individuals should not get cowardly because they get knocked down today.

What about her mistakes? Does anyone try to "kick her ass"? After mumbles from George Miller about hard asses, she laughs in her belly-shaking way, and says, "They've tried. Anytime they can do it successfully, they've got this office."

The capable Proctor is comfortably in charge. New York City competitor Frank Mingo says Proctor "has a tenacity, a single-mindedness, and is able to take a problem and concentrate on it, see it through—a trait necessary in advertising." Organized, intelligent, articulate, Barbara Gardner Proctor is her own best advertising package.

How did this woman develop these qualities, combine it all with an incredible drive, and succeed? "Way, way back in Black Mountain, when I was running around barefooted, ignorant... *and* black, in the South, Lena Horne was all we had.... My absolute super-inspiration for everything in this whole world in terms of what you can be and do was Lena. That was it. It was not her singing. . . . She would always take a stand and she was always dignified." In the late thirties and early forties, the jazz singer was her paradigm (and Joe Louis was the man that epitomized success to young black boys, says Proctor). Reading the *Afro-American*

Barbara Gardner Proctor

newspaper reports (shipped a week late from Baltimore) of this nationally known black woman who was also a lady, the young Barbara felt, "She was a classy chick. . . . I would like to think that some little kid has picked me out the way I picked out Lena Horne. If you can just influence one or two, then that's enough."

Today Barbara Gardner Proctor has personal friends of the caliber of Lena Horne, Jesse Jackson, Johnny Mathis, Charles Percy, Jim Brown, Nancy Wilson, Ossie Davis, Ruby Dee. . . . Yet she has little time for friendships. George Miller says, "Her priorities are two—her son and her business."

Barbara's son, Morgan Proctor, is a high-school student and, according to George Miller, Morgan "feels very much a part of

Proctor & Gardner." When the business was organized, the small child often slept under the conference table like a puppy while Miller and Proctor worked above his head. Interested in acting and magic—he recently auditioned for a movie—he attends public school across the street from his mother's office and often lunches with her. With his full lips and heavy-lidded eyes, he is coolly wary as he speaks with strangers, like a sleepy-eyed cat stalking a bird. One can feel his mind working behind those intelligent hooded eyes. His mother says that he is good at people-handling: "He's a terribly sophisticated child."

Barbara Proctor occasionally refers to teen-aged Morgan as "the baby." This son epitomizes the theory that it's the quality and not the quantity of time spent with the child that counts. The relationship between him and his mother is close, although Morgan feels she works too hard. Does she enjoy her business? "*Yeah!* She's just *always* going." Although she has a temper and yells, he admits, "She's reasonable sometimes... I guess," and adds that she's a bit too logical. Is she affectionate? "That depends on how I feel. When I want all of that..."

Although he does not remember Carl Proctor—who died recently in Manhattan—he is close to his paternal relatives. His mother is also in touch with the Proctors, her only family tie. She only visited her mother in Washington, D.C., to see her stepfather who has since died. Actually, the two Proctors are closest to Miller. When Barbara travels, George and her housekeeper share the responsibility for Morgan, who goes to George's apartment for weekends.

Barbara Proctor and her son live in a huge condominium filled with mirrored surfaces, trees in pots, hanging plants, and plush carpeting, and a panoramic view of Chicago from two terraces. She enjoys cooking large meals on Sundays; Morgan is an accomplished chef himself. Her way of relaxing is to collapse on her bed. They often go to movies on weekends, but "when it's been a *real* busy week she just relaxes." Yet if he suggests they socialize, she will.

Proctor does not vacation. "You only need a vacation if you need a relief from something you're doing. I enjoy it, so why do I need a vacation from it?"

With twenty-three employees—no one is sure of or cares about the ratio between races—and over six million dollars a year in accounts, Proctor donates time to, among others, the Chicago Black United Fund, the Girl Scouts, the Y.W.C.A., and the Boys' Club. She oversees the creative end of the business as well as the administrative. And because her business is intertwined with her personal life, her executive secretary runs personal errands in addition to attending to business affairs.

Always the business person, her five-foot-six, 135-pound image is what she's selling. "She keeps her nails nice, she's meticulous with her dress . . . extremely neat," comments her secretary. With no time to shop, she has her secretary select clothing for her to choose from or orders directly from New York. A fitter then comes to the office. Her favorite designers include Bill Blass, D'Angelo, Yves Saint Laurent, Steven Burrows, and Anne Klein. Although the flawlessly complexioned Proctor spends significantly on attire, an associate says, "She'll wear it and wear it and wear it." She prefers pantsuits and slacks for work and long dresses in the evening. She loves silk blouses; her perfume is Aromatic by Clinique. "We smell it all the time," says a worker. With heavy clunky gold diamond jewelry on her long shapely hands, she favors a special bracelet, each charm depicting one of her major accounts.

Well-groomed and impeccably dressed, the Proctor look includes children's ties purchased in boys' departments, perfect with her pantsuits.

She sported one of her little-boy ties recently during lunch at Maxim's, Chicago. With a French waiter hovering, Proctor is in control of the situation in the elegant room filled with Old World stained glass and deep-toned wooden paneling. She is a non-smoker and a non-gambler, and she drinks white wine. "I'm a Kentucky Squire," a member of the same Jack Daniel's Hard Drinkers' Club as Frank Sinatra, Dean Martin, and Jerry Lewis. "At the time they initiated me into that *great fraternity* [her voice is playfully sarcastic], there were only six women squires in the country." She states that if she were drinking it would be Jack Daniel's... "but I don't drink hard liquor any more." She "has an addictive personality," and prefers preventing problems to curing them—also her rationale for not getting involved with a man.

When she married, she was essentially the breadwinner in the household. "So I have never had—if it is to be considered a luxury, and I'm not sure it is—the *luxury* and *experience* of ever having to rely on a man for *anything*. In my entire life. I've earned it all or some woman has helped me to earn it." Proctor sees no reason to include a man in her life. She is not in need of male companionship. Years before, she faced the reality that the new baby, her own physical needs, and an infant company took all her time: "I'm not the kind of person who would have lots of light relationships. So that just precluded everything. I can't see how you can have a meaningful relationship with those blocks.... Where is the time? There is just no room.... People who ask me [about the possibility of marriage] usually ask from the traditional posture. And that is that marriage can provide for you financial security, travel, support, and services. And if that is the basis of marriage, then why should I? I have those. I need another reason. And any other reason would involve time. And all of mine is allocated. I don't have any more."

Question: But what about a desire for the sexuality of a man?

Answer: "What does that have to do with marriage?"

All her male relationships are business-related. Or Morgan-related. "Which is my other business. . . . I really don't have that personal need. I would much rather read more about Henry the Eighth." (An employee says, "I've seen the lonely side of her." In a melancholy mood Proctor once commented, "I think that I died back when I was sixteen when Johnny Welles left me.")

Proctor on spouses: "The hardest problem a woman executive has is that she does not have a wife . . . the balance to all the things which make the professional part go well. And if I had my druthers in terms of having to choose between a husband and a wife today, it certainly would be to try and find a wife.

"Corporate America tends to look at a wife as part of the corporate hardware. . . . They ask you if you have a driver's license, a car, and a wife. The wife is no more important than those other two things in terms of compensation. The wife has a perfectly legitimate right to be ticked off when these corporate husbands have got their jobs, maintained their positions, and elevated themselves through her support, and suddenly get turned on to the golden girl in the office and want to ditch the wife. Well, she *made* him, and somehow corporations and countries need to begin assessing the worth of a wife. And making that very clear in the contracts. A man should be penalized if he was hired with that wife and he divorces that wife. Well, hell, she ought to get part of his benefits that have accrued in the company. It seems to me that would be fair. . . . They expect her to keep up her home and do the corporate entertaining. And they expect Rosalynn Carter to go gallivanting around. Why should she work for nothing for this country. Why?" She advocates spouse-pay.

Proctor knows where she stands and what she thinks. If only her grandmother could see her as the successful human being she

is today. Proctor comments: "I think she does. I think she does."
Miller suggests perhaps a heavenly Coralee Baxter is the one who
bails them out of tight situations.

In an anthology of élite black Americans, Barbara Gardner
Proctor was the only self-made female included. All other
women either inherited or married money. She worked for her
success. Her grandmother would not be surprised; she always
knew her granddaughter had promise: "Not cute. But right
smart."

EPILOGUE

Reflections

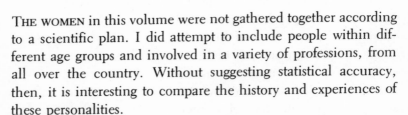

THE WOMEN in this volume were not gathered together according to a scientific plan. I did attempt to include people within different age groups and involved in a variety of professions, from all over the country. Without suggesting statistical accuracy, then, it is interesting to compare the history and experiences of these personalities.

Ranging from their thirties (Esty) to seventies (Clark), the women grew up and/or reside in Connecticut, England, Wisconsin, Texas, California, the Dakotas, New York, Florida, Oregon, South America, Minnesota, Colorado, North Carolina, and the state of Washington. Some were born the oldest child in their family, a few the youngest, and several in between. There is no only child. A couple are natural beauties, several are attractive, and others are plain, although all are pleasant-appearing, fine-looking people. Tall, short, heavyset, birdlike. One has a high childlike voice, while another speaks huskily.

Home state, physical appearance, and order of birth suggest differences, not similarities. Consideration of their life situations might be informative, without resorting to psychosociological pedantry.

Something motivated these women to eschew or to add to the traditional roles of wife and mother and enter the commercial environment. Since a criterion for inclusion in *Millionairess* is the lack of a financially secure background, it follows that several consciously meant to escape poverty-stricken childhoods. Others fled emotional adversities: Esty—with an unbending father—and her siblings all left home before high-school graduation. Proctor grew up in a shack with a slew of relatives. Both Vera Neumann's and Connie Boucher's fathers were Depression victims while Willis was sent to boarding school, staying through the summers. Clark's father died; she remembers her humiliation at the presentation of a charity food basket. The twins lived with a mentally ill mother. Conversely, the Frankfurt sisters and Ag Howard had stable home lives, as did Jean Rich, although Rich's parents were unreasonably strict. Nine of the twelve, then, had a difficult time emotionally, financially, or both.

Along with these expected commonalities and among numerous dissimilarities between the twelve, one curious pattern emerges. This collection of women brought together through their achievements are either the daughters of mothers who supported their broods without a husband's help, or the millionairesses themselves are single, divorced, or widowed, and count on themselves for monetary stability. Throughout two generations there emerges a lack of male dependence either by choice or by accident.

The traditional breadwinning father was absent from Catherine Clark's life after her twelfth year. Her widowed mother supported the family by doing wash.

Twins Jacqueline and Gillian lived with their divorced mother, seeing their male parent infrequently. The sisters themselves married in their late thirties after beginning a successful business as bachelor women.

The product of a divorced home, Beverly Willis saw her father when she was a teen-ager for the first time in over a decade. She has never married.

Constance Boucher, from a loving stable home, married, then divorced her husband, leaving herself with two sons.

Vera Neumann married late, then became a widow; she was left with a budding company and young children.

Elsie Frankfurt was single until long after she was wealthy and successful. Sister Edna's spouse took the role of mother as Edna became family supporter in the 1930s, which was unheard-of.

Teen-age bride Janet Esty divorced soon after she married, with baby Andrea to care for.

Jean Rich married, bore four children, then divorced her husband. She had no source of funds.

Agnes Howard is a widow, and childless. Before her husband's death she either lived apart from him in another state, supporting a beginning ranch, or ranched while her political mate frequently traveled.

The illegitimate Barbara Proctor, brought up in her divorced grandmother's home, met her father for the first time as an adult. After marriage, Barbara divorced as quickly as she deemed respectable, supporting her son, Morgan, by herself.

Child-support either was not forthcoming for the four who divorced or they refused to accept it. One said she wanted a clean break.

A group of females on their own, or the daughters of women who managed without a man. As of this writing, Agnes Howard,

Proctor, Willis, Esty, and Neumann do not reside with a male. One said, "I have never had—if it is to be considered a luxury, and I'm not sure it is—the luxury and experience of ever having to rely on a man. . . ."

Vera speaks of women who were homebodies, who never got out of the tea parties years ago; she and her eleven bookmates did manage to, one of whom admonishes females to stop rapping men for what women in fact do to themselves. Another feels American females are their own worst enemies, do not realize their own worth. Boucher, considering the paralleling careers of wife, mother, and businessperson, says it takes a woman more time to be an entrepreneur. And more energy.

Energy. Kipling said too much work and energy kills a man. The lives of these millionairesses imply, if he was correct in his analysis of male limitations, that it seems not to apply to women. One point emerged again and again at interviews. These females retire late and rise early. Whether their full lives are exciting and they don't want to waste time sleeping or they have higher than average metabolic rates and require less sleep is not known. It is clear that more hours per day to be striving toward a goal is helpful. These females seem to get a second wind when it is needed, no matter how overworked they are.

As for any group of achievers, the term "workaholic" crops up in discussions with and about them. Yet one insists work is not a dirty word, while another advises that you should rely only on yourself. "I couldn't sit still. I just couldn't sit home," states Howard. These females were allowed—and often, through circumstances, were forced—to make their own successes. Willis's "push them out" philosophy seems proven here. She also speaks of a gutsy streak, *chutzpah*, a strange courage.

Someone said to me it takes more than energy and enthusiasm to be a millionairess. I'm not sure. These traits are one unanimous link. Plus perhaps a certain necessary level of intelligence.

Within this collection of able women, some but not all are creative. Although Catherine Clark feels the key to success is to find a need, unexpectedly a number do not appear to be particularly innovative thinkers who invented an improved product or service. Energetic and enthusiastic, their prosperity seems either predicated upon or resultant in self-confidence, sure-footedness. There are other general similarities: They are all straightforward and although sometimes openly manipulative—Edna is an example—none are deceitful, that famed "female" characteristic. Decisive individuals who expect answers, they ask, "Do you want to do it or don't you want to do it?" And they take risks. Willis is a great believer in following clues and Rich talks of gambling when starting her business. "I decided, What the hell . . ." Clark feels it's imperative to recognize a chance when you see it. "If you think you can do something, it is a crime not to. . . ." These women have the courage to start, they dare to try.

And they follow through. Boucher says starting is fun, it's the long haul that is difficult. Agnes Howard, rancher, says one can do anything if one wants to badly enough, yet any of the twelve could have conceivably spoken the thought. All of them did say it, if not verbally then through their conquests, their mastery of their own lives. Willis talked her way into jobs with no training, the twins practically breezed into the tough show-business world; perhaps they bowled everyone over with their enthusiasm. Boucher bought contractual rights she knew nothing about, while Rich managed to buy an airplane with almost no collateral. Janet Esty is clearly a grubber and Proctor received the first service loan ever awarded by the Small Business Administration. These ladies don't sit still waiting for opportunities. Loaded with determination, tenacity, they do not discourage easily. They persevere; they're not easily knocked down. All consider themselves opportunists. There is a failing: they share absent-mindedness, probably a function of their busy, active careers.

Horatio Alger heroes. However, the self-made male of America is viewed as ingenious and delightful, and generally receives a positive image, while a different set of stereotypes is in play for the entrepreneurial woman: "pushy dame," "emasculating bitch," "a hard woman," "a driver," "cold, masculine," and the assumption that success is at the expense of her personal life and family.

These twelve women belie these preconceptions, for they are, for the most part, feminine. They share a state of womanliness as they produce in a man's world. Their female status is used to the hilt, although none offer their sex as an excuse for failure or difficulties.

Psychologists and sociologists suggest the high-powered woman requires a mentor for advice and encouragement. While no one achieves in a vacuum, it is interesting that most of the women did not feel the need for one particular individual to lean upon. However, although their mothers and fathers were not financial successes, in most cases the women had at least one supportive parent. (Beverly Willis, an exception, finally cemented a relationship with Louise Dillingham.) Janet Esty's mother recognized her daughter as an achiever, while her father believed there was no such word as "can't." A backlash reaction, Jean Rich showed her doubting parent she could "hack it." Boucher's parents saw Connie's ability and drive, and Proctor's grandmother said her granddaughter would amount to something someday.

Of the women in this volume, Barbara Proctor perhaps reveals the most unexpected dichotomy. The illegitimate child from North Carolina, the plain black girl who today is a classy woman, a beautiful person . . . How? Proctor's metamorphosis is perhaps not as amazing as it seems at first glance. She speaks of her grandmother as loving, affectionate; "beyond that she was extremely strong and reputable." With dignity and a sense of reality, Mrs. Baxter convinced Proctor she would excel. It would seem that money is often overemphasized. The necessary supportive positive elements of the making of the whole individual were present in that shack. Is it really so surprising that Coralee's granddaughter did in fact attain what she was told she would from her earliest days?

A mother, Proctor shared a dilemma with other ambitious females with offspring. Of the twelve millionairesses, nine have children. Three bore or acquired their families after they were rich and successful, and could purchase quality housekeeping and child care (Pollock, Neumann, and Baird); and Ravkind's husband, rather than she, accepted the maternal responsibilities. It is significant that Clark, Boucher, and Rich had mothers and Neumann a mother-in-law available to watch and love their children as businesses were established, thus eliminating motherly guilt and worry. Esty and Proctor are the two of the nine working parents who had to cope with the problems the care of a child entails.

Janet Esty's name originally caught my attention in a magazine article about successful females; I located the other eleven women in a variety of ways. While in Florida, I saw a Rich International *Airlines* news article including a photograph of the president. After I met Clark—whom I got in touch with after buying a package of Brownberry croutons—she sent me a piece about another woman. Friends, relatives, and associates provided clippings and gossip. My husband's co-worker knew someone in California. One lady was written up in *Fortune.* A call to a New York City architectural firm brought forth Willis's name. Locating Howard, buried in Dakota snowdrifts as I write this, required calls to editors of obscure Midwest agricultural papers.

With searching and digging I met them, and worked at understanding and knowing them. Pleasant, sociable, intelligent, and just plain nice, these females are the cream of America. I've repeatedly been asked which of the twelve I personally enjoyed the most. After weighing and thinking, all I can say is I like them all, each for different reasons. Knowing them has been one of the pleasures of my life.

ABOUT THE AUTHOR

LOIS RICH-MCCOY, born in 1941, was raised in Hollywood, Florida. The daughter of a self-made millionaire who migrated from Austria at the age of sixteen, Rich-McCoy attended Goddard College, where she earned a bachelor's degree in biology and a master's degree in science history/journalism. She worked in research laboratories in the fields of medicine, biochemistry, and marine geology, was a stock broker and owner of a small business.

She is married to an oceanographer who spent time at the Smithsonian Institute prior to working at Columbia University as a researcher and core curator. Dr. and Mrs. McCoy live with their children, aged 19, 18, 8, and 7, in a converted black barn in a hamlet on the Hudson River. The McCoys spend summers in Woods Hole in their homestead, "Old Bottles," named for the plethora of antique bottles dug in their back yard.

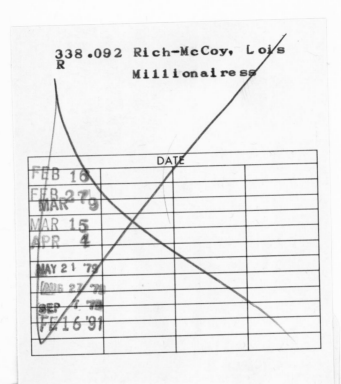

338.092 Rich-McCoy, Lois
R
          Millionairess

DATE			
FEB 16			
FEB 27			
MAR 9			
MAR 15			
APR 4			
MAY 21 '79			
AUG 27 '79			
SEP 7 '79			
FE 16 '91			